SEO Mastery 2025

#1 workbook To learn Secret Search Engine Optimization strategies to boost and improve your organic search ranking

Introduction

SEO (Search Engine Optimization) has to do with the science or process, and in some cases, the art of ensuring websites are well visible on search engines in results generated and get the maximum relevant traffic to the website. This is why "optimization" is used. This process involves so many more processes than anyone could have imagined, from the site's structure, the manner and way in which other websites connect to it, and the words mentioned in major areas of the site.

This knowledge is well-known and has been proven that the earlier and higher up a particular website is ranked or appears on search pages, the higher the traffic to be delivered by users of these search engines to that website.

Another factor influencing traffic is how frequent your content appears on result pages or the number of times that the website pops up on the results page of search engines. The main goal of SEO is to get the best of appearance as well as direct more traffic to a website through a search engine.

Search engines make use of Internet bots referred to as 'spiders' or 'crawlers' to help to index websites on the web and then ensure their indexes are kept updated. This process is referred to as crawling or to clarify better; crawling has to do with cataloging and reading websites on the Internet.

Note that SEO has to do with improving the natural or organic results generated by the search engines for one's website. What we mean by organic here is that these results are not optimized via paying search engines to do the job like those of ad-based optimization to achieve sponsored or paid results, which has to do with different tactics or strategies, and some payments made. Altogether, this is another process of search engine methodology.

Before we continue to explain the ways in which SEO achieves the objectives mentioned above for a particular website, let us consider a very important question: Why is SEO necessary for a website to begin with? Read this book to free yourself from the myths and errors that can ruin your website. Let’s get started!

1. Introduction to SEO

What is SEO and How does it Work?

Search Engine Optimization or SEO for short, does exactly what the name says it does; optimize websites for search engines. It combines a number of different strategies, procedures and actions that are used to increase website traffic organically (in other words, unpaid) by tactically placing the website in the highest possible position in search engine results.

Ranking highly on search engines is very important as the majority of web traffic comes from the largest search engines (Google, Yahoo and Bing). Nowadays, the majority of web users use search engines as their main point of contact to websites as search engines group all the possible, different and most relevant options on one page just like a super powerful yellow-pages book.

So if you rank high on these search engines, your website will get more targeted traffic that will be more exposure for your brand image, business, product or cause. In this guide, I am going to be covering all the basic principles you need to implement to flood your website with visitors and in return, achieve your website's desired objective.

How do Search Engines Operate?

Now, the key here is the high ranking in the search engine, so it would be fair to say that the search engines play the main role in the success of our websites. Therefore, I think it is right to assume that understanding how they operate is a fundamental point. Below, I am going to explain in very simple terms, how a search engine works.

In a nutshell, search engines have three main tasks: Crawling, Indexing and Providing Answers (aka 'Searching').

1. Crawling and Indexing

A beautiful thing about the internet is the billions and billions of nuggets of information available to us at a click of a mouse. For the most part, the days of spending hours in the library, going through books and files to find the answer to a simple question are now gone. Today, research time has been reduced to milliseconds through easy access to information on our laptops and smartphones and most importantly, due to the power of search engines.

"How do they do it?"

Well they use 'Crawlers'. Crawlers or 'Spiders' are automated robots created by search engines to collect data from billions of web pages, pdf files, photo files, the whole lot. These bots are sent on spy missions to go through all the data flying all over the internet and their job is to read the code, look out for the most important indicators of the page's content (title, subtitle, meta tags, etc.) and store this information as well as its location.

2. **Providing Answers**

   The overwhelming amount of data that is stored in numerous worldwide databases is then processed in milliseconds to provide answers to internet browsers searching for an answer, particular file, topic, etc.

   When someone searches for something, the search engine uses the indexed data to give the searcher the best result possible. The crawlers go back into action and bring forth information that is popular and with relevant words, titles, tags, etc. that best match the keywords searched.

This is a very simplistic explanation but nevertheless gives you a very good understanding of the functions of search engines. I must say that nowadays, search engines have become smarter and have more complex algorithms where only the fittest websites survive.

A question people commonly ask is:

"Why do I need to do anything at all then?"

or

"Why don't the search engines that are so advanced, take care of everything for me?"

Well, as advanced and as powerful as they are, search engines still require some assistance from you. There are thousands of new websites going live every day and many in your target niche, so it is in your best interest to make the job as easy as possible for the search engines and ensure they collect as much information about your site as possible.

By taking the right actions and optimizing your website the right way, you are giving yourself a massive advantage over other websites in your target market and attracting thousands of visitors to your website, versus the competition. If you fail to take SEO seriously, you are literally limiting your success and missing out on huge opportunities.

For this reason, it must be your number one purpose to understand all you can about this topic and to put the information in this book into practice so that you may achieve a sky-high ranking and never-ending traffic for website. With SEO, you will help the engines locate and provide your content to relevant users.

Apart from search engines, there are also search websites called directories. These websites are similar to search engines, as they allow users to find particular services by searching, however the way they display sites is different. Like we discussed, search engines use algorithms and bots that go all over the net looking for webpages that match particular searches, but with directories, everything is done manually. They have a team of people that search through the internet looking to find new websites and that are also responsible for reviewing websites that would like to be featured on their site. People doing this manually means that users will be assured that the websites featured are of high quality.

Though less popular, directories can still be a good source of traffic for you, but just bear in mind that your website will have to stand out immensely from others to be featured. Also, you may have to pay an administrative-fee to be featured on a directory site.

The First Step to Ranking in Search Engines

As you can probably begin to tell from the last few points, SEO is not rocket science. There are a few components that will get a website ranking high and I have dropped a few hints already. However, before we discuss in detail what those tactics are, we must first get your website in the search engines and give you an extra boost by helping the search engines help you.

If you followed the simple step-by-step instructions in my best-selling book:

"WORDPRESS: Simple WordPress Guide to Create an Attractive Website or Blog from Scratch, Step-By-Step", then you have probably already setup a well-functioning website that has an appealing appearance and that is full of relevant and original content. If you have not, don't worry! Now it is time to actually submit our website to the search engines to make the ranking process quicker.

The first step to ranking on search engines is to **manually submit your website to different search engines!** Manually submitting is recommended as it will less likely mark your site as spam when appearing in search engine results. The more search engines you submit your site to, the easier it can be with ranking in the results. For this example, we will focus on Google as it is responsible for 67% of the world's searches, but we will be addressing different search engines throughout the book as they are important too. There are different ways of submitting to search engines depending on what kind of content you are offering. For website submission, the simplest way is by submitting your URL.

Here Are 3 Simple Steps:

1. Visit **http://www.google.com/addurl**. You will need a Gmail account to continue. If you do not have one, it's recommended you create one)

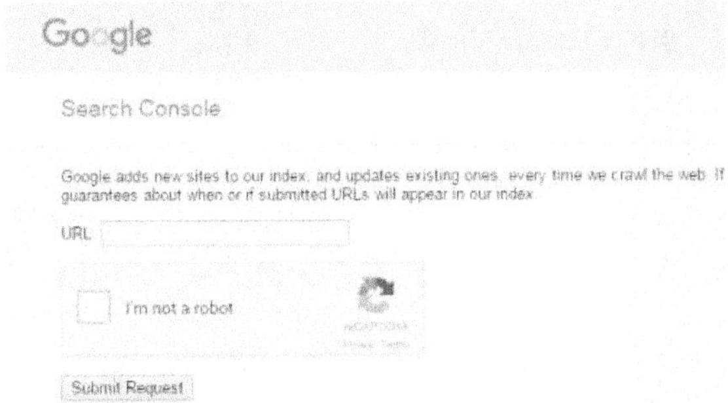

2. Simply copy and paste the URL you created for your website into the section marked 'URL.' Be sure to include the whole link so it will appear as http://www.YourURLHere.com/ in the box.

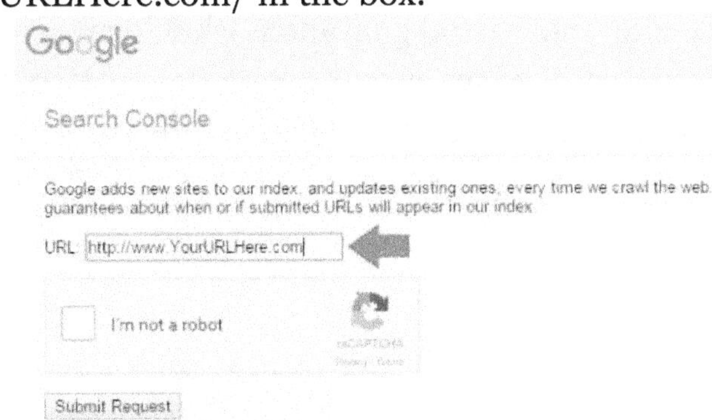

3. The last step here should be to click the verification icon and then hit **Submit Request**!

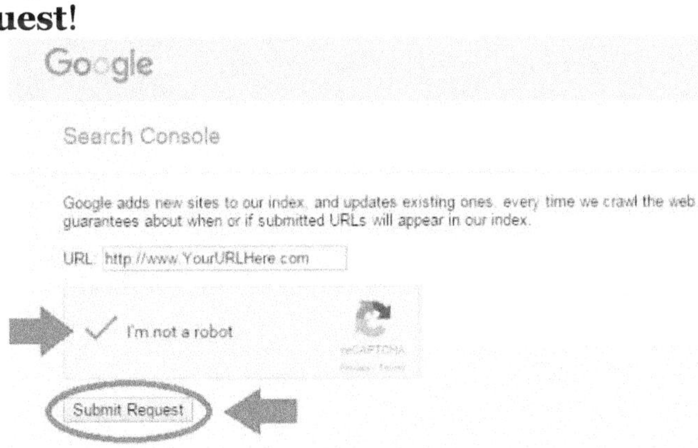

Your website has been submitted to Google search engines! You are on your way to getting your site out there! So far so good!

As mentioned before, it is best to do numerous submissions of your site's URL to as many search engines as possible to get maximum exposure for your brand. For other search engines to submit your site to visit:

www.fast-traffic-seo.blogspot.com

This site includes several search engines that you can pick and choose from, as well listing different submission techniques for those search engines!

Another great website to find the best free search engines and directories to submit to is:

www.freewebsubmission.com/

So your site has been submitted! Are we done? No, not quite! Even though we have now submitted our site, there is no guarantee when or where your website will appear in the search engine results since it will take a day or two before it is completely submitted, but even then it's unlikely to be ranked very high. Nevertheless, this is great progress!

2. Why Should You Care About SEO Anyway?

Okay, so SEO is a way of helping to make your company get more visibility online, but aren't there any other ways to do that?

While PPC (pay per click) advertising and social media campaigns do have their place, there are many reasons that SEO rises above the rest as the best way to increase your online presence.

Here are 5 reasons why you should care about SEO if you don't already:

1. It works

First and foremost, SEO works if you're doing it correctly. In the hands of the right people, a great SEO strategy can increase your website rankings in Google, get you the clicks you're looking for, and make your business more profitable than before.

As Joshua Guerra, CEO of the marketing firm BIZCOR explains: "As long as you are focusing on optimal user experience while performing methodic SEO strategies, you will be rewarded with higher rankings and organic traffic."

2. It's cost-effective

If you're always worrying about funds and budgets, you'll be happy to hear that SEO is generally very cost-effective. SEO is almost always cheaper to orchestrate than PPC advertising, social media advertising, purchasing email leads, and a wide range of other online marketing strategies.

Search Engine Optimization tends to have a very good ROI, and you don't need a ton of upfront capital to invest in it - you just need to hire a good team or consultant that knows what they are doing.

3. It increases your brand visibility

Every brand needs to maximize its visibility to its customer base; otherwise, what's the point?

SEO done correctly can help to bring your brand to an internet user who may not have been familiar with you before. If your small candle-making business comes up when someone searches "independent candle shops" in Google, you have an opportunity to hook in a new customer.

It's also worth remembering that **80-90% of consumers** look at online reviews before making a purchase these days, whether they're in a store or shopping online. If a customer goes to search for your business and can't find you, it reflects poorly on your brand.

4. It builds credibility and trust

If you have a website with good content that is well-optimized for SEO and a positive user experience (UX), then you're going to build up credibility for your brand. This is especially useful for young companies that are trying to get a foothold in their space and establish themselves as a reputable brand.

If a customer can find your website easily, and this generates a fast-loading website full of valuable content, you start to look more and more trustworthy. If done correctly, you build lifetime customers this way.

5. Your competitors do it

Even if all the other reasons haven't convinced you that SEO is a great investment for small businesses, then face the reality that your competitors are already doing it.

If your competitors are investing in SEO, but you're refusing to give it a try, they will slowly begin to steal potential customers from you just because they're just much easier to find.

Using SEO helps you to stay in the know about the latest business practices and makes it easier for you to stay on top of competing businesses in the never-ending search for customers.

If you're not investing in SEO, your competitors will. Once a company has ranked #1 for your keyword of choice, you now have 1 more competitor to compete with – and it's only going to be increasingly much harder for you to catch up.

SEO can make or break your business in the digital age, so make sure you take it seriously!

5 SEO Terms You Need To Know

Yes, there are a lot of terms you need to know when starting out in SEO, and understanding it all can seem a little daunting.

Nonetheless, here are 5 important SEO terms that you need to know for a foundational understanding.

1. SEO

SEO stands for "Search Engine Optimization." This is a set of techniques and processes used by an SEO Specialist to improve your website's rankings in the search engines for a particular set of keywords, or keyword phrases.

Of course, the real goal is to increase targeted website traffic in hopes of generating new business. This is achieved through better search engine rankings. Studies have proven that the **top 1-4 listings** get far more traffic than the rest of the results.

SEO techniques include things like properly optimizing your website content for target keywords, making your website fast/responsive for mobile, and getting backlinks from other websites to rank higher in Google search results.

2. Keywords

Keywords are the basis of any SEO campaign. Keywords are essentially short words and phrases that people type into Google when they're trying to find your business and related products/services that your business can help them with.

SEO specialists optimize content with keywords peppered into the sentences, as this helps Google to understand what your website is about and helps it to rank for the relevant keywords.

For example, if you are a plumbing business, Google wants to see plumbing related content on your website. So ideally, your website should have keywords like plumber, plumbing and other relevant terms to help Google understand the nature of your business.

3. SERPs

SERPs stands for "Search Engine Results Pages." Basically, it's the page that is returned to you whenever you use a search engine.

When we talk about "getting to the first page of Google", we're referring to the first page of the SERPs.

The goal of SEO is to improve your web page's ranking amongst the other "organic" listings in the SERPs.

In the context of internet searches, "organic" traffic is when people find your website through a search (rather than through an ad).

4. Algorithm

You're going to hear me talking about algorithms an awful lot in this book. In an SEO context, an algorithm is a set of instructions that Google uses to decide what it's going to show you when you type a keyword into it.

There are way too many webpages for a human to look through all this stuff.

The Google search algorithm is very complex, and often the people who design it don't even fully understand it due to machine-learning processes where the technology finds the most effective way to do things without needing human intervention or strict instructions.

Google's search algorithm is always being updated, so it's important for SEO specialists to keep up with the latest changes and algorithm updates. The way that Google decides to rank search results can change instantly with an update.

5. Backlinks

Defining backlinks is a challenge only because there are a variety of other terms that mean basically the same thing. You may also hear them referred to as **text links, anchor text links, hypertext links, one-way links,** or **contextual links.**

Put simply, a backlink occurs whenever another site links to yours.

The link could come from an image or banner type graphic, or it could be a linked phrase of text, known as anchor text. For SEO purposes, the text links are of primary importance, with the goal being to get links using keyword phrases you are trying to rank for.

While there are hundreds of other SEO terms to learn, these will give you a good framework to build upon. Whether you are learning more so you can improve your own site or just want to be able to communicate better with your SEO Specialist, I encourage you to keep studying.

3. Understanding Search Engines

How Search Engines Work

Though search engines are majorly just Internet navigators, it would be very unrealistic to imagine the existence of the Internet without them. As a result of the absolute depth and size of the World Wide Web, this handy information becomes unusable and meaningless without the presence of search engines. Basically, three tasks are performed by search engines:

- The use phrases of specific words in searching the World Wide Web
- The results found as well as their locations are indexed
- User access is offered to this index as well as the ability to search for it making use of combinations of desired phrases or words

Search engines today perform about ten million queries each day, and they constantly evolve and reinvent their services to go in line with the needs of advertisers, users, and websites.

It begins with something referred to as spiders (also known as crawlers) and how great, knowing fully well that the Internet is referred to as the World Wide Web. Spiders are referred to as robots or inter-bots made up of coding or software. Internet spiders, just like real spiders do something referred to as web crawling or simply crawling to make a long list of whatever is found on the Internet.

Crawling is referred to as an act of copying, indexing, and browsing done by the spiders. They begin with a well-known website (the web's busy part) or a heavily used server and then crawl outwards to whatever link is found on the server or website behaving just like real spiders when they spread.

Though Google was the first to bring up the spider idea, using this has become well known across the community of search engines, and the desire is always to create newer, more creative, and faster spiders.

Everything we read is indexed by spiders, making use of something referred to as metatags, which are explanations of phrases or keywords under which the owner of the website would like the indexing of his or her website to be done. They assist these spiders in understanding what the page deals with and where it can be located in an index.

Webmasters may utilize descriptions or words in metatags that are not accurate or reference well-known keywords and topics which may be difficult for their website to handle. To fight against this, spiders are brought in to correlate these metatags with website content and then come up with an understanding of where the page should be on an index.

Another large organ in search engine anatomy is the algorithm used. Algorithms have to do with computer coding or software designed to take those words inputted into the search bar and then deliver results that are most relevant from the indexes made by these spiders. They turn search engines into an answering machine. They depend on clues or signals from websites indexed to come up with search result rankings.

These signals vary in the freshness of the content on the website, the number of times it was visited recently, and that particular region where the user is making this query belongs. Google is known to make use of about 2000 different signals in assisting its algorithms in the creation of search listings each time the search button on the computer is tapped.

How Users Interact with Search Engines_

The secret to designing as well as improving any service or product is considering the human aspect of the interaction of real people with it. If there's a need to come up with a marketing strategy that focuses on search engine marketing and SEO, it starts with understanding the way and manner in which users interact with these search engines. Users can only be given what they desire if you have an idea of what it is, and what they are getting already and how best you want to improve on it.

Search Engine Figures and Facts_

Let us begin by having some understanding of some figures and figures about people and search engines, so we have an idea of where we stand. As of 2011, about 59% of Internet users utilize search engines on a daily basis, which is just about an inch of the most used Internet application as of today, known as an email that accounts for about 61% of users on a daily basis.

This tells us how the dominance and reliance on the activities of search over the activities of other Internet are on the rise. As revealed by StatsCounter, the largest market share is held by Google, sending about 91% of traffic, followed by Yahoo! at 3.78% and then Bing at 3.72%.

UserCentric also carried out a study demonstrating that users tend to concentrate more on organic results compared to sponsored or paid results, and there's a higher chance to click organic results compared to sponsored results. Interestingly, advertisements, as well as sponsored results, tend to get equal and, in some scenarios, get more attention when they pop up first in organic results.

Another discovery from this study was that users tend to pay little or no attention to what is found at the bottom of the page compared to what appears on top. The same way, descriptions, and keywords that are written in bold tend to receive more attention as well as click-through rates compared to just simple text, most especially if it is located below the page.

Search Engine Marketing (SEM)_

SEM, which is also called search engine marketing is an Internet marketing that deals with the promotion of websites and making them more visible by either the website structure themselves and optimizing the content and how they perform in search engines, or by making use of advertising and buying sponsored results. The final goal is getting higher rankings in searches, be more visible, and gain some new traffic while keeping old users. This has turned into a big market in itself. In North America, about $19 billion was spent by advertisers on the Internet in the year 2012.

The greatest vendors of online marketing with search engines are Bing Ads, Baidu, and Google AdWords. Agencies majorly for advertising have started specializing in SEM due to the fact that this form of Internet marketing is growing very fast and even surpassed some traditional types of advertising. Though, the majority of campaigns are performed through agencies and vendors, SEM tools and self-serve solutions can be found online as well. SEM has now covered a wide range of marketing activities that are related to search engines, which include managing sponsored listings, submitting websites to directories, and creating marketing strategies to ensure the success of organizations, individuals, and businesses operating through the web.

Marketing through search engines has to do with:

• Natural or organic results: The improvements of these results are made possible through search engine optimization; this is exactly what we are talking about in this book.

• Paid results: Here, advertising programs are utilized in the promotion of websites in result pages of search engines.

Therefore, marketing using search engines has to do with different tasks that will promote the website, whether they are paid or organic results. Below are some significant tasks involved in the whole process.

Keyword Analysis_

This has to do with analyzing keywords in order to find relevant keywords, which are responsible for the greatest traffic for a service or product. For instance, making use of studio flats or keyword studio apartments will be made based on the activity involved in keyword analysis as well as how to trend on the Internet.

The Popularity of the Site_

This has to do with the measure of the presence or weight carried by a website on different search engines. This is measured by search engine saturation, which indicates how much indexing is performed on a given website by spiders and the number of backlinks present on a website.

HTML Tools and Web Analytics_

This refers to the website's backend or the invisible part of the website to users. It includes web analytic tools that help in measuring, analyzing, and logging file analyzers to other complex ones such as page tagging that makes use of an image or a JavaScript to follow users' actions on a page. Spider-simulators and HTML validators are tools that function in optimizing a site's hidden areas for issues as well as those regarding usability. They ensure that all pages conform to the code standards of the W3C.

Sponsored Results_

This deals with purchasing places or purchasing advertisements on pages of search engines to achieve higher views in the section of sponsored results and involves the PPC (Pay-Per-Click) solutions that are provided by the search engines.

Why is search engine marketing important?

With the Internet, there's a unique quality in e-commerce over other traditional business forms, and this is how it is based on new, creative, and entertaining content as well as reduced startup costs. You only need a great idea as well as little cash to start making some money on the Internet.

To be successful in any Internet business, it entails attracting a large number of visitors to a website, and this can only be possible when you deliver great content and make it very accessible to a large number of users. All websites and businesses on the Internet are usually struggling for the best visibility.

Here are the reasons why SEM is so important these days.

First, everyone makes use of search engines, as discussed earlier, to the extent that it is already becoming the Internet's most popular activity. This is why it is the major battleground for the resources and attention of Internet users. With SEM, your website is taken out of your hands and then set in front of a large Internet community – the users of search engines.

Users of the Internet have clouded their minds with the idea that businesses or websites that don't show up on search engines are not legitimate. No website can have this legitimacy factor unless it engages in SEM and is visible on search engines.

With SEM, you are free to do whatever you like with your page because your site can be self-supporting through the income obtained from traffic. There's no need to sell anything. You can have a website or blog about any topic of your choice or offer any service desired without getting worried about giving support to the website.

SEO and SEM are advertising forms that are available to all and can be used in promoting your website without getting any assistance from anyone, or you can request the services of a professional or an agency to help you in this regard. The optimization and marketing will just continue itself if it is properly done and regular enough, so far, your contents are still on the web and in a particular location.

Lastly, if you're an Internet organization, public individual, business, or interest group, you can be very sure that any of your competitors out there are involved in both SEO and SEM.

4. Keyword Research

Before you even start considering building your website, you should perform a general search of relevant keywords in your particular niche or target market. Following the famous 80/20-principle (where 80% of the results come from 20% of the effort put into something), the act of keyword research is the 20% for achieving SEO results.

Many different methods exist of performing proper keyword research, but I'll explain a very basic and easy (and free) way of finding relevant keywords to target. The tool we will be using for this is called the Google Keyword Planner.

Google Keyword Planner

What better place to check if a keywords gets monthly searches than using Google's data itself? That's why the free to use tool Google Keyword Planner is perfect for keyword research. Admittedly, using the tool is somewhat of a pain sometimes, but at least it's a great free alternative to tools like Long Tail Pro (which have a monthly fee).

The Keyword Planner is actually part of Google AdWords, which is the tool you can use to create paid advertisements on Google's search engine for specific keywords.

Finding the Keyword planner can be complicated because you need a Gmail account to be able to use it, and go through a little maze to find it. Here's the steps:

- Type in 'Google Keyword Planner' in Google
- Click top result
- Log in with your email data
- Register if needed (only once)
- Navigate using the top menu to 'Helpful Tools'
- Click on the keyword planner
- Set your targeting range to your preferred nation you wish to target with your website
- Add your keywords that are somewhat related to your niche in the 'Your Product or Service' box at the top.

The results should look something like the image below. You can choose from Ad group ideas, which are clusters of keywords related to what you entered in your keyword box, or you can look for specific keywords using the tab called 'keyword ideas'. Average monthly searches might no longer be very specific, these have been switched with an estimation.

Logic dictates that you wish to select high search volumes with low competition. However, you may also want to go for low volume search keywords with high competition, if there's a buyer intent behind a certain keyword (such as 'product X review' or 'best product X 2017'.

Understanding Keywords

There's a real science behind choosing and understand what keywords to choose for SEO targeting. Whilst most of this will come from simply doing and having experience with what works and what doesn't, here's a few beginner's directions. By following the tips below you will be able to better understand which keywords to choose.

Know your niche

What problem are people trying to solve when they look for your website? What products do these people want to buy or what information would they like to know? Understand the needs of your target audience. Once you have a clear view of what your audience would like to know or have, that's when you can start looking for keywords related to that.

Go for long-tail

It's pretty normal that the search terms you're trying to show up for have a lot of competition. That's why it's a good strategy to adapt your keyword research and go for longer phrases people are typing into the Google search bar. These types of keywords are referred to as 'long-tail keywords'. And of course, these words need to be specific to your website topic.

Check competitiveness

This goes back to the previous point: don't try to rank for keywords with high competition. Focus on the low competition ones, preferably those with a lot of people that are looking for those keywords. If you have barely any competition, it will be much easier for your new website to show up high in the Google search rankings.

Make a clear overview

When you do keyword research, open up an Excel sheet (or similar) and write down ALL keywords you have found in a list. Mark the most important ones and also write down the competition level, search volume and some additional thoughts about the keywords you found (for example which category they belong to). A clear mind and good research starts with good documentation. Having an overview of your keywords does that for you.

Know What Your Competition Does

A simple strategy I like to use is to actually go out and see what other websites are doing. Obviously, I will only look at the websites that are ranked at the top for the keyword I'd like to be number 1 at with my own website.

There are numerous tools that will allow you to identify the keyword strategies for certain websites, but in my experience the one that has worked best is called SemRush (it's an expensive SEO tool). So if you're serious about this SEO thing I highly recommend you to take a quick peek at what they allow you to do.

You could also just get a quick website analysis by looking at the Sitemap of a competing site, or run Xenu Link Sleuth (a free software tool) to see what links and pages a competing site has got going on. The idea is to 'borrow' the keywords your competitors are using, because these have obviously worked very well to get their site to the top of Google.

5. On-Page SEO

Now we know what keywords to target, it's time to break down the act of 'doing SEO' on your site. It's not really complicated at all, but you need to know what components to address. In general, SEO is made up out of the following three elements:

- **On-Page SEO:** Using site-relevant keywords in your website pages, so Google can determine the relevance of your site for certain search terms. Determined by (in diminishing importance): page or post titles, URL description keywords, outbound links, links from one page in your website to another, image alt texts, embedded videos, H1-title tags, and relevant content text keywords.
- **Off-Page SEO:** Gathering relevant backlinks to your website, preferably with good anchor text diversification. This means that the links that point to your website have been placed with relevant keywords in them, but not in a manner that makes them look spammy in any way.
- **Social SEO:** This element of SEO is becoming more and more important recently. Having consistent social media activity supports your on- and off-page SEO and will be the secret sauce on top of your ranking efforts. Social SEO means to place links to your site or articles from social media accounts with high power to them. These could be Web 2.0's, or similar.

Optimizing Your Website

The optimization of a website is performed using good on-site SEO. Generally, people who do SEO will be building their site using WordPress, which allows them to install SEO plugins in order to track the on-site SEO performance.

Recommended plugins to track SEO are called 'All-in-One SEO Pack' and 'Yoast SEO'. Both work equally well, but have different systems to them. It's a matter of preference. If you wish to learn more about WordPress and SEO, please consider reading my other book on WordPress website creation.

Forging A Perfect SEO-Optimized Page

Quick disclaimer: I do not promise you this will work for you. I do not promise you this will even work tomorrow. But this is what has worked for me, and what works right now as I write this book. I'm positive at least some of this will continue to be relevant forever, so hopefully this will help in your own SEO optimization process.

Let's try to forge the perfect storm for a basic page on your website. What can you do to optimize it so Google will love it? Let's look at the on-page SEO factors in diminishing relevance. We will take the example of a bakery website that's trying to rank high in Google for the keyword 'Chocolate Donuts'. On the next page you can find what such a page COULD look like. The layout, however, does not matter one single bit for SEO purposes. So do not be afraid to diversify.

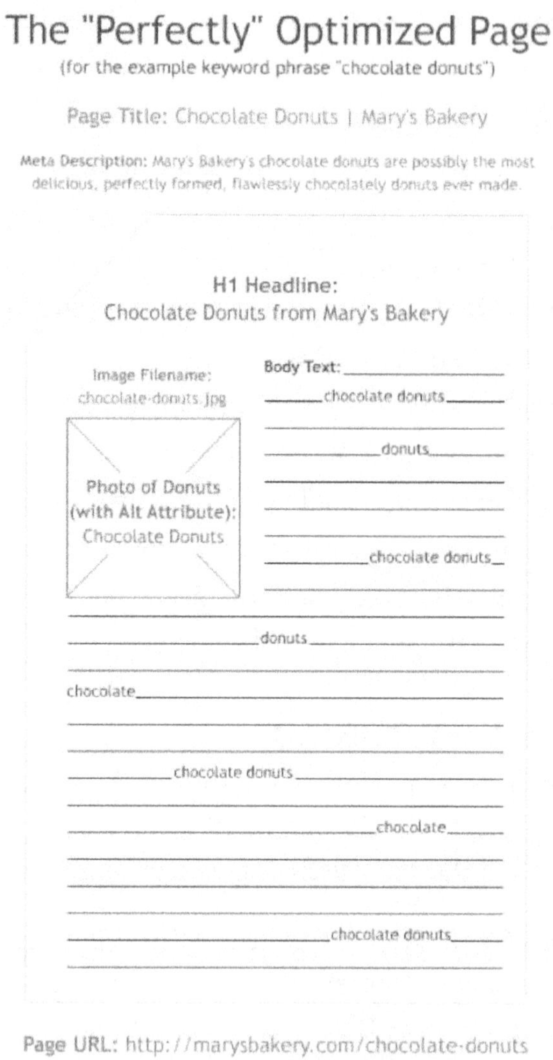

Page title (H1 Headline)

Obviously, your page title should have your exact keyword in it, preferably the very first word(s). Keep the title as short as possible, no keyword stuffing. Also place your exact match keyword title in your Meta Description Title (which happens automatically sometimes). This is the little blurb that you see showing up when you search for websites in Google.

Page URL keyword

In the example, we target chocolate donuts. But our website is called www.marysbakery.com. Make sure that your URL is as short as humanly possible. You can adapt this in the website setting if you're working in WordPress. For our example site, the most ideal situation for SEO purposes is making our page URL: http://marysbakery.com/chocolate-donuts. And nothing more. Then it's perfect if you are targeting chocolate donuts. The key is to place your exact match keyword directly behind your domain URL. And no other symbols, letters, numbers, or unneeded nonsense. Keep it clean.

Meta description

This is one of the most important on-page SEO elements that is technically 'off-page'. Because the Meta description for a page will not show up on your website, but on Google. The description is nothing more than the little blurb of text you see under a page link, when you search for something in Google. The trick is to place our example keyword 'chocolate donuts' at the front of the Meta description title, but also at least once somewhere in the description text. I highly recommend to also include a synonym or similar word to your keyword in your description text, because Google's algorithm will pick up on this. Don't just dump or stuff keywords, but make it a coherent piece of text that someone is eager to click. It's like a tiny sales letter for your page, on Google.

Outbound link to authority site

This is omitted from the example image above, but extremely important for SEO. Add an outbound link to an authority website (a website that is deemed super powerful) which is relevant to your keyword. For example, our chocolate donuts article would at least link one time to a Wikipedia article about 'Chocolate Donuts'. Or a news article on the BBC website about 'chocolate donuts'.

Inbound link to another page on your own site

Interlinking is extremely powerful to help your other webpages on the same website giving each other a boost. Place at least one link to another page on your site in the content of your article. For example, if you have a related article on your site about 'vanilla donuts', link to that with the anchor text 'vanilla donuts'.

Image Alt Attribute(s)

You can at keywords to your on-page images that you embed in your content. These so-called 'alt attributes' can be placed using HTML, or in WordPress by changing the media content. Just place the exact match keyword ONLY ONCE in one of the images (so the alt-attribute will be 'chocolate-donuts' with a dash)

Embedded video (optional)
This will help boost your site even more, but is not necessary all the time. Embed a YouTube video with some traction (a bunch of views and interaction such as likes and comments) that contains your focus keyword. Preferably, this is an exact match keyword.

Body text keywords
Throughout your article, place the exact match keyword, but (very importantly) also variations of this keyword, in your overall text. The example image above shows exactly how to place these keywords throughout your text. It's very important to not force this placement, and simply write your text like a normal human being would. Just make sure you use your keyword at least once or twice. DO NOT overdo it, this will be seen as spam and will seriously harm your SEO for your page. Despite what some so-called experts claim, there is no real rule to when it is 'too much'. Just focus on providing value to your readers and don't spam your keyword, is the takeaway message here.

Relevant Factors Influencing On-Page SEO

There's a multitude of factors that will improve your website's SEO performance in Google's eyes. We will go over them one by one, and give a short explanation. As time progresses, these may become more or less important, as SEO is a dynamic thing, just like the internet itself.

Interlinking
This has already been touched upon, but it is very important to link between relevant pages on your own website quite often. This way, the link power will flow between the pages, making them stronger in the process. Google will see this as a positive thing and will consequently give you better rankings.

Website Speed
It's very important to keep track of the loadings speeds on your website. Logic tells us that better loading speeds of pages will give you better SEO results. Google provides website owners with a simple to use and understand free tool to track what to improve with regards to website speed. You can find the tool here and simply enter your website domain name to get the results: https://developers.google.com/speed/pagespeed/insights/.

Responsiveness
This basically boils down to the fact if your website design is suitable for mobile users. The internet is increasingly moving towards mobile platforms: smartphones and tablets. The majority of the traffic already comes from these sources and is only projected to grow. No wonder that Google deems it extremely important that your website design is

'responsive'. If it's not, fix it immediately. Not having a website design suited for mobile or tablet will completely obliterate your ranking results.

Safety

What's relatively new in the SEO space is the need for an SSL-certificate on your website. This is basically only visible in the domain URL – it will show an https://-protocol instead of the regular http:// ones. Having an SSL is beneficial and will be increasingly important as time progresses. Not only for the privacy safety of your visitors, but also for SEO purposes. Your website host is able to give out an SSL-certificate for your site. Sometimes this will cost you a monthly or yearly fee, but in today's internet that's more than worth the investment to get that competitive edge from your competitors.

Website Age & Size

This one is difficult to influence and will come with time. The older and bigger the website, the more authority Google will give to it. As your site gets older it will collect more backlinks and more domain authority. That's also a reason why expired domains are so popular in the SEO space.

Topical Relevance

Having a very specific niche topic to your site, and sticking to that topic throughout your entire site, will be extremely helpful to determine what the site is about, and consequently will help you rank your site for niche keywords in your specific target market. Staying topically relevant and sticking to your topic is thus essential for some good old Google rankings.

6. SEO & Link building

Links are perhaps the best kept secret of benefiting from SEO. You are aware of their importance for Google, and how they affect the rankings in the search results. This section is your 'how to' section, that will explain everything that you need to know about links and developing them in order to get the desired results.

Consider that you are looking at two products, X and Y. You have purchased product X before and you know that it is of high quality and can be trusted. You have never tried product Y before, and so far, don't know anything concrete about it. If the maker of product X recommends that you give product Y a try, then you will, because you trust product X. You do not expect to be misdirected. The same concept applies when it comes to SEO and links.

When one-page links to another, the suggestion is that the other page is recommended. This makes it easier to drive traffic to that page. That is why the more that this occurs, the more Google decides that a page can be trusted and deserves a high SERP.

If this piece of information makes you want to secure as many links as you can to your site from other sites, you need to take a moment, and look deeper as there is more to discover. It is not just the link itself that is important and taken into consideration, where the link is placed carries just as much information. There are sites that have tried to create a number of dubious links so that they can improve their search results, but these are shut down before they can have any real effect. It is better to have four links on high ranking sites than to have a thousand links on sites which are not trusted.

Types of Links

There are two main types of links that you can take advantage of for SEO purposes, and these are expressed links and implied links. Expressed links are those which people are able to click on so that they can interact directly with your website.

However, it is worth noting and understanding what an implied link is. This is a link where your website receives a mention, usually in an article or blog post, but there is no direct link on this mention that a reader is able to click on. Even without having a clickable link, the mere fact that your website has been mentioned in this way is an indication to your search engine that your website is increasing in its popularity, and reveals that people are willing to talk about what you have to offer. For the search engine, this reveals a perception of importance and touches on your overall credibility. In order to provide content that is relevant for those who are searching, implied links also have an effect on SEO results.

Find a Link Target

Since the placement of your links is important for link building, you need to find the right link target where you place your link. A link target is a page that is aligned with what you have to offer, so that when people are looking for information, they will see your link, believe it to be relevant and click on it. The actual process of finding this is quite simple.

Begin by exploring the sites that do something similar to you. This could be the sites that you visit often for information, or those that are competing with you at some level. For example, if you are selling second hand books, a good link target would be a site that is selling discounted gift items. Using your personal judgment to identify this site is quite possible the best thing that you can do, although there are search engine tools to help you if you need the help. The reason personal judgment is great is because you know what you want to be associated with for the benefit of your website and your product.

Once your link has been featured on that site, then you have succeeded in building a link which is able to send you valuable and targeted traffic. This will improve on the reputation on your web page, further elevating you in the ranking.

Establishing your Links

You have found your target, you are enthusiastic about building that link, but there is just one problem. The site that you are targeting is well established and highly popular, and cannot understand why they need to link with your site. In fact, they may be facing a situation where they receive hundreds of requests to link on a daily basis. In this scenario, what often happens is that they may attempt to get you to place a banner advertisement on their site. This will get you some coverage, but you will not experience the benefit of SEO that a link can provide. Therefore, you need to be creative when it comes to link building.

Go back to basics and create some excellent content. Make sure that this content is highly relevant to the site that you want to link to. If possible, mention this site within your content such that anyone who is reading will also be encouraged to look at the other site. You must put in all your effort to secure that valuable link, including embedding video or other creative tools into the content that you prepare. If you approach the site that you want to link to with this well thought out strategy, you will find that they are more likely to want to link with you. Furthermore, it shall also be revealed that on your site, there is an opportunity to create a link to them as well.

Other Ways of Getting Your Links

The aforementioned method is challenging, but the best way that you can get the links that you need. There are other ways that you can try to build up some links. The simplest way, which can sometimes be effective, is to go to a link seller. This is not the direct

SEO approach, but it can help to ensure that there are some links. This will make a difference in your rankings, especially if they have been very low, but it is no guarantee that you will make it to the first page of the search results. This is because the links that are built from a link seller tend to be low in their overall quality, and as the search engine recognizes them for what they are, they typically stop working, and you may be forced to continue paying for them.

Another option that you can use is writing of articles, where you capitalize on SEO to get the results you desire. This will need you to use keywords which are guaranteed to generated traffic. This enables you to get some traffic though the overall quality of the links remains low.

The next thing that you can attempt is using social media to leverage your links. If you have the intention of increasing the overall traffic to your page, then social media will do this for you effectively. What you need to be careful of is the aggression with which you execute your campaign, as if you do not do it well, you create spam, which could work against you instead.

There are two ways that you can try to improve your SEO, and these include taking the slow and steady approach to doing it yourself or maximizing on short term returns by employing a company to do it. The option that you choose will be solely based on what you want to achieve. What is worth noting when it comes to link building is like with SEO, it does not have to cost you anything. Paying for this as a service does not guarantee that you will get better results. What it could do in the long run is negatively affect your site with the search engine criteria, such that you find in the long run your ranking is even lower than you have anticipated. The best way to benefit from link building is to have information that is worth linking too, so it goes back to ensuring your content is of the highest quality. When you maintain this consistently, it is your site that will make it difficult for the site with poor quality content to get a high ranking in the search results.

What you Should Avoid

Without realizing it, you may be taking certain actions that are damaging your chances of a high ranking from search results. In fact, some of the things that you are doing may cause you to have no presence on search engines as if your web page is invisible. Here are some actions that you need to avoid if you want SEO to work for you.

Purchasing Backlinks

With all the competition that exists online, you may be tempted to capitalize on methods that appear to be worthy shortcuts. One of these is purchasing your backlinks through a range of websites online. This is a move that you should avoid at all costs for two reasons. First, it is highly possible that the site you are purchasing backlinks from will get shutdown by Google or any other search engine. The second reason is that once Google or other search engines realize that you have purchased backlinks to capitalize on SEO results, your own website could end up being banned as well.

Keep Away from Frames

These were a popular way to create a web page, and they include a browser window that has been divided into at least two frames, with each frame catering to a web page. These are challenging to view on mobile devices, meaning that for the most part they are not responsive. In addition, they are not well handled by most browsers, so people find it difficult to access them when needed, which affects their overall ranking.

Frames also affect the way that pages appear in search results, which can interfere with the links to the pages. When there is a page that has been framed, in a search it may appear as though it the segments within the page are independent pages, as this is the way that they are likely indexed. This makes it impossible to have a link which sends people to a specific page on your website. What happens is that if there are any links from other sites, they only lead to the front of the site or the home page, and are unable to go to specific sites.

The complication becomes clearer when you consider that on a framed page, you will have more than one URL as each frame will have an independent one. When someone puts in an inquiry in a search engine, what happens is that they are unable to get a proper response, unless they know the actual URL of the page that they are looking for.

Local SEO

Almost all web pages have the letters WWW before the name of the web page. This stands for world wide web. The words indicate that placing any information on the internet opens it out to scrutiny all over the world. However, when you are seeking customers, what you should aim to accomplish is having all the information available in your local area, so that you can benefit from significant growth.

The reasons that local SEO is growing is because there are more people using smartphones today. This means that they are better connected, often looking for information when they are on the go. This is different from the normal SEO results that you would have as the information that you receive in the results is more actionable.

For example, consider you are looking for the best shoe shop in your area. If you type in the best shoe shop in the search engine, you may get information on shoe shops all over the world. If the search engine is able to narrow down on your location, then the information that you receive will be highly relevant, and the results will be for the shoe shops that are within your area.

As someone who is looking to drive people to your website, consider this. Someone is looking for information on what you have to offer using their mobile phone, and they want to reach the nearest possible person so that they can get what they need immediately. When you include local keywords within your content, then it is possible to get a localized result. The way that you use this is also important if you want to get excellent results.

One thing you can do is maximize the benefits that are made available on Google. This can be done by going to Google places which enable you to create a business page. On this business page, you are able to put in vital information about your business, including your contact information, hours of operation and physical address. In addition, you can place your website under a specific category, making it easier for people to find you. What all this does is optimize your placement when people are searching for information. Normally, when searching for a phone number, for example, the first results you will see take on the appearance of business cards at the top of the search results. These are the results that are generated from people who have created their business pages. In addition to providing this localized information, it is also possible for people to locate you more easily using a map.

The next thing you must do is create a strategy that will elevate your rankings by focusing on your on-page optimization and your off-page optimization. You must use the right format for your business, for example when providing information on your address, so that it can be easily found when a search engine is used. This information should not be restricted to the contact us page. If you visit any good SEO site, you will realize that this is the type of information that you will find on either the header or the footer of every page on the website.

When looking at off-page optimization, you must find other sites in your local area that you can place links on. If you cannot place links, you can try and get a citation on these sites. This is an interesting way of using SEO to elevate your site in search results. Places that are highly popular for citations include review sites, such as Trip advisor and Yelp.

The Key Differences between Local SEO and Global SEO

The reason that it is important to look at local SEO on its own is that it is different from global SEO in some essential way. To begin with, in local SEO, most of the information that elevate your ranking on a site comes from information that you provide on the actual site. Content is essential. However, when you are focusing on local SEO, particularly if you want to do this for your business, then your focus shifts and is placed on the information that you provide for your business through Google.

In addition, Global SEO places focus on the creation of backlinks which help increase the reputation and authoritative nature of the website. This normally means that it is legitimate and therefore worth referring to. However, with local SEO, the focus shifts to citations which are the mentions that your website or your business will receive when it appears in business listings. In this case, your site will increase in rankings if your customers have a positive outlook towards it.

Remember that there are many search engines out there where you need the power of SEO. Make sure that you create a viable presence on all of them.

Getting the Content Right

Just because you are focused on providing information on your physical address to get rankings, does not mean that you should completely forget the value of high quality content. The content that you provide must also be highly relevant so that the customers in your local area are able to find it. Consider the titles that you use for example. Perhaps you are a Thai restaurant and you are based in Dallas, Texas. When creating a title or header for your web page, you need to factor in all this information in your content. This would call for you to have a title such as 'Siam Thai Restaurant, Dallas Texas'. This means that when the search engine is looking for your information, it will be much easier to identify and place you amongst Thai restaurants that are based in the area.

Therefore, ensure that the content that you have on your website is able to address who you are as a business. In addition, it also should talk about what it is that you do, and the reason behind your core purpose. Finally, for the best SEO results, it should be clear where you are located.

Building the Perfect Site

Therefore, what else can you add to your site to take the best advantage of Local SEO? To begin with, ensure that any user that lands on your site is able to find a variety of ways that they can get in touch with you. This means that your contact information should be visible, and on as many pages as possible.

In addition, if there is information that a customer may need to go away with after they have reached your site following a search, ensure that this information can easily be stored by making it possible to download it. This would include information on your pricing as well as lists of the products that you have available for sale.

Finally, your site which has local SEO should make it possible to create an appointment for your services, or to prompt a callback. This makes your site functional, meaning that more people will access it and have something positive to say. The final result of this will be an elevated ranking on the SERPs.

7. SEO Tips for Marketing Your Startup

Getting SEO right is particularly important for the startup business. Marketing today is nothing like it was 10 years ago, and even 2 years ago, to be fair. So much has changed in that it is no longer easy to get past the search engines and become successful without having to consider SEO, and how it will work in relation to your website. If you choose to ignore SEO, you might as well pack up and go home now.

The Internet has a brand new face and with that goes the need for a completely new strategy in terms of developing SEO campaigns that work, in order to keep your website in the eye of the search engine spiders.

The top 10 SEO tips for getting your startup business noticed are:

1. Work out your target keywords

Good SEO research begins with keywords. To determine your optimal keywords, you must carry out an in-depth analysis of search trends, current and recent past, as well as taking demographics into account. You are looking for target keywords that will give you the most amount of return with the least amount of competition. You need to get your readers interested in what you are writing and publishing and, as any good content marketer will inform you, this is the very first step to building up a relationship with your target audience. Of course, as we have mentioned before, you also need to make sure that readers don't notice the repetitive nature of keywords in your content, to avoid a marketing voice to anything you publish on your site.

2. Make your website mobile friendly

This really is absolutely necessary if you want to get anywhere in today's mobile world. Having a mobile friendly website is the new standard and that has been completely backed up by the latest update from search engine giant, Google. However, the biggest mistake that many website owners make is in thinking that they have to completely re-build their website to make it usable on mobile devices - this simply isn't true. There are lots of ways to convert your existing website into a mobile friendly one without spending a vast amount of money to do so. Even if money is a concern of yours, not making your site mobile-friendly will cost you far more than it will to make it mobile.

We spend so much time on our phones that of course, whilst people are sat on the bus going to work, or sat waiting for an appointment, they are going to sit and peruse the Internet - make sure you don't miss out on this money-making scheme.

3. Keep it simple

When you create content for your startup, you need to be able to make a strong connection with your audience. The best way to do this is to keep things simple - put your message across in a nice, simple way, and in a readable way. At the end of the day, many of the people you are talking to are not going to be industry experts and, if you use too much technical jargon, you will lose them very quickly. In the ideal world, your content will read simply enough for someone who has no background in the industry to understand it perfectly.

The best test of this is to ask someone else to read what you have written, before you go live with it. This person needs to have no knowledge of your service or product, to give you the ideal test of whether your content is relatable.

4. Develop a proper marketing strategy and follow it

A good marketing strategy will let you set an end goal to work to, with other goals in between. It will take your target demographic into account, the number of blog posts or social media posts you are going to do each day or week, what your content is going to do, and you can then solve problems when your content does not work as you expected it to. Marketing strategies are never set in stone; they will constantly move, the goalposts will change and you must be ready to move with it. Before it can do that though, you have to make the development of your marketing strategy plan one of your very first jobs. Don't be too rigid, allow yourself to make mistakes, but always ensure that you correct them afterwards.

5. Use the power of infographics

In the last few years, infographics have grown to become one of the most popular forms of media used in content, and they are also one of the most popular forms of content shared on social media sites. The reason for their success is very simple – infographics are incredibly powerful, using both graphics and text to grab the attention of the reader and pull them into your content. The combination of the two is far more powerful than either one on their own, so always make sure you take advantage of this.

6. Get your priorities right

The single biggest mistake that rookie businesses make when they set up their marketing strategy is not getting their priorities in order. No matter what your business is, the most important facet, the most important resource that you have, is time. In order to be able to manage your time effectively, you have to be aware of what needs to be done first and then balance it with what is going to have the most impact on your target audience. There really isn't anything to be gained from doing something in a highly efficient and effective manner if it didn't need doing in the first place; don't waste time, because time certainly is money.

7. Work out which social channels you will use

There are so many social media channels that it can be difficult to work out where to go to get the best impact. Some people fall into the trap of trying to use them all and find that, as per the above point, their most important resource is being used up on things that really are not necessary. A little bit of research will root out the best channels for you to use, the ones where most of your target audience spend their time - that is where your attention needs to be directed. We talked about the most common social media sites to use previously, so choose these main ones, and then filter through the others accordingly.

8. Build your links

These days, link building requires that you have a proper understanding of how things like anchor tags work. You also need to have a solid understanding of how to use them to raise your search engine ranking. One of the keys to working out which websites are the best ones to link to is to work out link relevancy. There are plenty of tools, free and paid, that allow you to see very quickly if a link has any benefit or is any good; this is vital because the links that you choose signify your websites' relevancy to your particular niche. Using a tool such as this also saves time wasting and potential costly mistakes.

9. Your content must be relevant

If you are producing content about a specific topic within your niche, you must do everything necessary, everything that the topic is covering. Your content is what is going to attract new users to your website, so keeping it high in quality and completely relevant is going to stop your website from stagnating. This also gives weight to the idea of generating high quality backlinks that go with high quality content and, together, all of this makes for a good rank on the search engine page rankings. On top of this, any images you use must speak about the content you are writing about; nobody is going to have trust or confidence in a business who simply throw images at content, which has no relevancy at all.

10. Analytics really are your friend

Numbers do not tell lies, and the numbers that are relevant to you will tell you all about your website, which bits are successful and which bits aren't. While it is important to celebrate the successes, you must never ignore the failures. In truth, these numbers are probably more important because these are the ones that help you to see where you are going wrong, and give you valuable information to indicate where you can improve your website. Analytics give you some good goals to work towards, and are an excellent guide to whether your marketing campaign is working as it should be. Don't get too downcast when you see an area that is failing; turn this into a positive and see it as an opportunity for improvement.

The importance of a good quality website

It is all very well and good talking about SEO, and what you should and shouldn't do, but if you don't have a top quality website to promote in the first place, what is the point of any of it? We are going to talk about this several times across this book, and we will reiterate each point a few times also, which should tell you a lot about how important it truly is.

If your website is full of broken links, it's boring to look at, hard to find your way around, and basically doesn't give the customer much information, then you're not going to find visitors heading back to your site once they've looked at it once; you're certainly not going to get any shares or likes on Facebook, and people aren't going to give you that all important word of mouth promotion either.

Can you now see how important it is to give some serious thought to your ground work? Let's head back to the basics.

Okay, so you want to promote your goods or services through the medium of the Internet.

Good choice. Everyone is online these days, whether they want to be or not, and this literally opens up the world for your business. In order to keep people visiting your site, and to avoid them turning off completely, here are a few tips to follow:

Make sure the format and design reflects your business. Yes, you might want to go all colorful and fancy, but if your product or service isn't really about that, then you're basically not understanding your own niche, whilst also confusing your customers in the process. Choose a design which says something about who you are; if your product is fun and light-hearted, go for a colorful and fun design, if your product is more serious, go for something which is a little more formal. It's all about knowing who you are, so you can easily inform others.

Write down what you want to have on your site. Too many pages and nobody will ever navigate their way around them all, too little and you're not giving enough information. Have a brainstorming session and write down the key pages you need to have on your site; these should include:

- An eye-catching front page - this could show current promotions and sales advertisements.

- About Us – Tell your customers a little about who you are and what you do, including how long you've been doing it.

- Testimonials – Everyone loves to read about an experience a former customer has had with your business, so make sure you ask happy customers to leave you a review; this will drive future business your way.

- FAQ – Everyone also love to have their frequently asked questions answered, so make sure you think about this and compile a list of things which you are asked regularly. Make sure your answers are comprehensive and actually answer the question, without going around the houses.

- Contact Us – A regularly checked email account address, telephone number(s), postal address, and links to your social media accounts, including Facebook, Twitter etc. You could also have a section here which allows customers to submit questions to your site – you can download a widget for this quite easily.

- A blog. Blogs are powerful tools, and they speak to your customers on a personal level. You could have your blog actually on your website page, or you could link to it; basically whichever works for you, however having your blog actually on this page cuts out the messing around for your customers.

- Your actual product information. This could be your online catalogue, whereby customers buy their products, or it could be in-depth information on what you sell/provide.

Make sure all your links actually work. It's no good have links to different parts of your website, or even external links to other sites, if they don't work when a customer clicks on them. Think about this from your point of view – how many times have you clicked on link and found it broken? Did you go back to the site again? Or did you get frustrated and simply give up and go somewhere else? I'm guessing you went somewhere else, which is what your customers will do if you don't check your links are working regularly.

Update your site regularly. If you have a blog on your site then you need to blog around least twice per week, however don't do it too much because otherwise it gets too repetitive. In terms of your front page, make sure you update this regularly too with new offers and news. If your site is stagnant for too long, people will forget about it, and nobody will go back to it. Forgotten websites do not drive sales forward.

If you have no idea how to build a website, get someone else to do it for you. Yes, you can save money by doing it yourself, and it's quite easy to do too, but if you have no idea where to start, and you're not really sure what you're doing, it's false economy to drive forward in a DIY manner. You can easily hire a freelancer to design and build your website for you, making use of their specialized skills to help you create a strong and powerful site for future use.

Equally, if you don't have the time to maintain the site, you could hire a virtual worker to do your website work for you. The pros of this are that you don't need to actually hire them in a conventional way, i.e. you don't have to provide a desk, computer, pay for electric and heating etc, because you hire them online, as a freelancer, in a virtual way. This frees you up to work on other parts of the business, and again, you can make use of specialized skills, which you might not have.

Cut out the waffle. If you build pages and update for the sake of it, with no real aim to the whole procedure, then your customers are going to see straight through it. Make sure everything you put on your website it concise, and make sure you actually have a voice. By this, I mean that you are speaking to your customers in the same way every time – don't use the first person for one update, and then switch to the third person; be consistent and your customers will see this as a genuine person speaking to them. Any content you put on your website has to be of a high quality, because any errors in spelling and grammar will be picked up on, and this is a huge vote of no confidence for customers. How many times have you read something on a flyer or website and picked up on a mistake? Did it leave you with a feeling of confidence? I'm guessing not.

Put simply, you could have the best SEO plan in the world, but if your website isn't up to scratch, there really is no point in going ahead with it. Combine your SEO efforts with a top quality website and you really are on the road to success.

8. Using Your Brand to Boost your SEO

An often overlooked way of boosting your position in the search engine results is to use the profile of your brand. This may even be something that has already built up significantly but that you have not tapped into yet. In fact your brand name can help to boost your SEO is several important ways:

Direct Traffic

The largest share of traffic to your website is likely to be organic. This is people who have searched on a specific subject or keywords and your site has popped up in the results. This is what most people think about when they consider search engine optimization. However, although this can be responsible for between a third and a half of all your traffic, direct traffic is the second biggest with social media links following just behind.

To utilize the power of your brand you will need to mention it naturally as frequently as possible in all your marketing campaigns and social content. This even applies to direct marketing. The idea is that if a person is exposed to the name of the company frequently it will stick with them so that when they do need something you have to offer, your brand name will be on the tip of their tongue.

The difference between this and general searching on the internet is that you will either enter the web address exactly, or very closely. Your use of a specific brand name will make your search results much more specific and ensure potential customers can easily find your site.

Building a brand name is a little more complicated than simply adding your name into a social posting. People need to learn what your brand name stands for; this is not just what the product is, it is also the attributes of your product. In effect you need your brand name to link in someone's head with a quality product or a quickly dispatched product. Whatever it is that makes your product unique is the key to ensuring people remember you and return to you by searching on your brand name not a general phrase.

Google Algorithm's

Not everyone realizes that Google, and the other main search engines, actually look at brand recognition when complying results. This is done by monitoring search results and which links are selected. If there is a tendency to search for a particular brand and visit your site, or if people are on your site and searching for something specific the search engines will notice the frequency that this occurs. Once this level has passed the requirements of the search engine provider then it is likely that your website will be designated as one with 'brand authority'.

Of course, this is not the only part of the search equation. The number of back links still plays a vital part in securing a high spot in the results. Google will compare the number of links with the number of brand searches; the higher the link level the more brand authority will be given to the site and the better your site will feature in the search results.

It is important to note that brand marketing can be completed offline a well as online. If your budget can stretch to it then TV and magazine advertising can be an excellent way to get you product in front of people and start the process of brand recognition. If brand recognition is not something that your competitors are doing then it will take very little effort to become a brand authority. Google will always rate those who have product branding higher than those who do not; the more branding you do the better you will appear in the results. Of course, this process does take time; you cannot change your brand authority overnight!

Improved links

It used to be simple to construct a link between your business and another online one; you could simply ask or pay for a link to anyone. The more links you had the better you would appear in the search results. However, this was changed a few years ago and now only links which have been genuinely earned and are relevant to your website are counted. It has, therefore, become more difficult to create new authentic links; it generally involves writing press releases and hoping various online and offline publications will post the release with a link to your site. Alternatively respected bloggers can be asked to complete a review to create a link.

Thankfully, if you are thorough about your branding you will already be creating a product that people relate to and are interested in. If you look after your brand then other sites will be interested in connecting with you; this will take far less effort on your part and still enable you to obtain excellent results.

Monitoring

One of the most important things that you should do regularly is monitor the social media sites and any other mention if your brad or business. This could be described as a PR exercise but it is also an important part of using your brand to boost your SEO and, ultimately, sales.

It is no longer necessary to troll through the internet every day in the hope of finding your brand or website mentioned; there is now a variety of software applications which can do this for you. Simply install the software or app and follow the set-up instructions. You will then be able to check your results daily.

The software will flag up any post on the internet which is relevant to you and your brand. You will then be able to assess the impact of this on your current sales plan and you may need to take action to ensure any potential damage is dealt with quickly. Monitoring the internet will also allow you to understand what is being said about your brand and what improvements need to be made. You will then be able to follow through on this and implement any changes to ensure your brand is perceived the right way; this will encourage sales.

An additional benefit of the monitoring tools is that you should be able to track your competitors. This will allow you to see what they are doing which you are not and which items you are doing better than them. You will then be able to use this information to improve your own brand.

The Algorithm

The best way to ensure you are at the top of every search is to know how the search engines compile the results; you will then be able to do exactly what is necessary to be at the top of the search results! Unfortunately, it is not that easy, if it were, everyone would be doing it! In fact, no one knows the exact algorithm which is used by the search engines, but the following elements play an important part. Maximizing your use of these will ensure you are near the top of any listing:

- Content

Put simply the more relevant the information is to the search that someone may perform, the better your results will be. The best way to achieve this is to focus on as many smaller, segmented pages as possible. Each page should deal with a specific subject. The search engines will realize that you have a page which is orientated to a specific subject and will list it higher in the results. This is especially true if you manage to create a page which is optimized in the view of the search engines; customers will be directed there as it is a relevant page for any search in a specific term.

- Linking

This has already been discussed in the context of improving the number of quality links you have by improving your brand awareness and attracting other businesses to want to link with you. As mentioned, this is an essential way to build a customer base as well as improve your search engine position.

Creating links also has an additional benefit, the more links you are able to establish the easier the search engines will find it to index and understand your entire website. This will help you to appear in the results for a wide variety of related subjects as the search engine robots will be able to index your entire site and link people directly to relevant material. To maximize your sales from this improved linking you will need to have a call to action on each of your pages.

- Your website

The search engines work on authenticity and legitimacy. Links and good content will all help to improve this. However, one of the simplest principles, which are often overlooked, is to have your own website. This means a website which contains the business name. Using generic websites which have common addresses, such as '.freesite.com' will not help you to create the feeling of authenticity to the search engines. It is also likely to make it harder to create brand recognition as your brand is not part of your address. Buying your own domain and hosting your site is not expensive and is a valuable investment.

Your own domain also helps to inspire trust and confidence from your customers and may encourage people to your site simply because they feel you are authentic.

9. SEO Techniques & Strategies

As we've discussed in depth, SEO is a way to attain high rankings in organic search engine results. SEO should never be the sole means of marketing any business, because search engine algorithms are in constant flux, and any one of (on average) daily changes can impact a website's ranking negatively, to a point where the entire business can be put in jeopardy. So, organic rankings should never be the sole source of traffic for any website that is being run as a business. With that said, SEO can contribute greatly to almost any online marketing campaign.

SEO is a long-term process, especially if it is to contribute in a tangible fashion to the bottom line of an online marketing effort. It is a mid- to long-term solution which does require time to produce results. So, if you have just started an online business (or one that has an online component) and are looking a way to jumpstart your website traffic, SEO is not for you.

There is often a misunderstanding in what an SEO campaign can realistically accomplish. As stated multiple times, SEO is not magic, nor is it an exact science where an action will have a specific and completely predictable reaction. No SEO company can produce high rankings for its clients by simply offering directory submissions, and half-witted articles written by college dropouts who hire out their writing skill so unscrupulous SEO companies for pennies per word.

While most search engine companies try to keep their processes a secret, their criteria for high spots on SERPs isn't a complete mystery. Search engines are successful only if they provide a user links to the best Web sites related to the user's search terms. You must find a way to show search engines that your site belongs at the top of the heap. That's where SEO comes in -- it's a collection of techniques a webmaster can use to improve his or her site's SERP position.

Experts in SEO can tell you the steps you need to take to be one of the top entries on a SERP. In an ideal World Wide Web, your site would rise to the top of every search engine's skydiving SERP based on content alone. While it's possible for your site to take the No. 1 SERP spot on its own, it could take months or even longer. Even worse, there's no guarantee your skydiving site will ever make it as high as the first page of search results. For some webmasters, site traffic isn't that big a deal -- their sites might be a personal project. But for anyone who uses the Web to make money, it's crucial. Whether the webmaster makes money by selling products on the site or through hosting Web advertisements, more visitors translates into more money. That's why some large companies are willing to spend money on SEO consultants -- they can be a worthy investment if the company's site is ranked higher than competitor sites.

SEO techniques rely on how search engines work. Some are legitimate methods that are a great way to let search engines know your Web page exists. Other techniques aren't good ways to get noticed and might involve exploiting a search engine so that it gives the page a higher ranking. Sometimes it's tough to tell if an approach is legitimate. If it seems a little questionable, it's probably a bad idea.

To fully understand and successfully adapt SEO in the business' marketing framework, the company should adapt the following strategies in order to obtain the best results:

1. Optimize for mobile search and browsing

Mobile optimization has been important for years. However, in October 2016 mobile overtook desktop with mobile and tablet accounting for 51.3 percent of all web browsing. Around this same time (November 2016), Google launched their mobile-first index. Previously, Google crawled the desktop version of a site, using that as their primary search engine index. However, with this update, Google has now started to use the mobile version of a site as its primary index. This means prioritizing your mobile site and mobile content is a must.

2. Engage in intentional link building

Links have been the most important driver of rankings for years now. Google has confirmed they're one of the top three ranking factors (along with content and Rank-Brain), and multiple ranking factor studies have confirmed this. A recent study from Stone Temple seems to indicate that links are even more powerful than we thought. However, they also found that links alone aren't enough to redeem low-quality content. Their advice, "If your content is not relevant or competitive, links won't help your ranking. If it is, links will make the difference."

3. Optimize for voice search

According to KPCB's 2016 Internet Trends Report, voice search queries have seen more than a 35X increase since 2008 and more than a 7x increase since 2010. The report also cites Andrew Ng, Chief Scientist at Baidu, as saying, "As speech recognition accuracy goes from say 95% to 99%, all of us in the room will go from barely using it today to using it all the time. Most people underestimate the difference between 95% and 99% accuracy - 99% is a game changer..." It's only a matter of time before we hit that 99% mark. Prepare now by optimizing your content for voice search.

4. Optimize for Rich Answers

As of 2015, Rich Answers were displayed for nearly 20% of all queries. This number is likely to be significantly higher in 2017. If you want your content to show for common industry-related questions, it's vital that you intentionally optimize for these queries. There are many ways you can do this, including explicitly asking the question in your content, including a direct answer followed by more in-depth backup info, using lists and creating Q&A pages.

5. Consider using shorter URLs

Using descriptive, keyword-relevant URLs has been an effective SEO strategy for years. However, some research seems to indicate that using shorter URLs may lead to higher rankings. While there's no set number of words you should include, Google has indicated in the past that anything after the first five words won't be given as much credit. Whenever possible, use your primary keywords in the first few words of your URL, and try to keep your entire URL to around five words total.

6. Local optimization is a must

Given the move toward a mobile-first mindset, it's no surprise that many experts are placing increased emphasis on local search these days. If you have a local component to your business, optimizing for local search in 2017 is imperative. As more of your customers turn to mobile to find local businesses, products and information, getting found for local keywords is a must.

7. Focus on improving user experience

We've known for years that providing a good user experience is the key to rankings. However, the connection between user experience metrics (click-through rates, bounce rates, etc.) has always been a indirect one. There is a direct connection between high rankings and beating out the expected CTR of other pages in the SERPs. In other words, if your content shows up in the SERPs but doesn't outperform the other results in terms of clicks, you may not hold onto your rankings for long. One of the most important things you can do to ensure your CTRs remain strong is to optimize your metadata for your chosen keywords. Remember: Your title tag and meta description act as your ad copy in the SERPs, and should engage viewers and entice them to click-through.

8. Use related keywords in your content

Keyword research is still a critically-important aspect of SEO. However, it shouldn't just be about finding one or two words or phrases to use in your content. Ideally, look for phrases that are semantically-connected to your main topic. For instance, if I'm writing a blog post about making a black forest cake, I'll most likely need to use words like "cherries", "chocolate" and "whipped cream." Using these words will prove to Google that I'm comprehensively covering my topic. It will also mean I have a much more balanced and detailed article -- which is great for user experience.

9. Write longer content

It's not only content length that leads to increased rankings but content quality: The goal isn't to simply write 2,000 words of rambling content. No, size matters, but so does the quality in that size. It needs to be well written for starters, and it can't go off on tangents. The content must be laser-focused. Anecdotal evidence aside, virtually every study done to date shows a correlation between longer content and higher rankings. Some suggest 1,200-1,300 words, while others say 1500 words should be the minimum. If you want your content to rank, I suggest aiming for a minimum length of 1,200 words for standard blog posts, and 2,000 words+ for evergreen content.

10. Speed up your site

For years, Google has been emphasizing the need to have a fast site. However, considering the upcoming mobile-first index, I imagine site speed will become an even more significant ranking factor in 2017. In September, Google again emphasized the importance of speed, particularly in relation to mobile devices: "Slow loading sites frustrate users and negatively impact publishers. In our new study, “The Need for Mobile Speed,” we found that 53 percent of mobile site visits are abandoned if pages take longer than 3 seconds to load."

11. Aim for high topical authority

If you're writing long-form, comprehensive content there's a good chance you're already achieving this. However, it's too important a strategy not to explicitly spell out. In a recent analysis of 1 million search results, Brian Dean of Backlinko found that comprehensive content vastly outranked more shallow content. He even found that pages that comprehensively covered a topic outranked shorter content that was highly-optimized for a certain keyword - even when the comprehensive page didn't use that keyword at all.

In other words, focus more on the depth and breadth of your content rather than on word count and keywords. This will undoubtedly be better for rankings as well as user experience.

12. Focus on user intent

Since the one-to-one relationship between keywords and rankings is now gone -- or is at least significantly diminished -- optimizing for intent is even more crucial. This will mean focusing not just on specific keywords, but on the meaning and motivation behind those words and phrases. What are people looking for when they use those queries? What long tail phrases should I be using to attract highly-relevant visitors? Which keywords should I focus on to drive conversions and not just traffic?

SEO Services and Usability

Website SEO Audit

An SEO audit can come in varying levels of detail and complexity. A simple website audit can be as short as a few pages long, and would address glaring on-page issues such as missing titles, and lack of content. On the other end of the spectrum, a comprehensive website SEO audit will be comprised of dozens of pages (for most larger sites it will be over one hundred pages) and address even the tiniest of website elements which may potentially be detrimental to the ranking-ability of a website. With a basic audit, a website owner should expect to receive a well thought out guide for not only fixing elements of the website which are not search engine friendly, but also guidance for going beyond addressing issues, and making marked improvements in areas of content, link development, and overall organic search strategy. It is important to realize that even though having a search engine friendly website is the first crucial step towards attaining improved rankings, there is no guarantee that the implementation of recommendations from an SEO audit will catapult a website's rankings to the top of search engine result pages (SERPs). SEO results take time, and require diligent maintenance in order to produce reliable and stable rankings.

On-Page SEO

On-page (sometimes called on-site) SEO is the process of implementing the necessary changes as recommended by an SEO audit. These changes can be implemented by the website owner (if they have the capability) or an SEO company. On-page SEO should be part of all SEO packages, as it is the foundation up on which a successful SEO campaign must be built. On-page SEO addresses a variety of fundamental elements (as they relate to SEO) such as page titles, headings, content and content organization, and internal link structure. As with a website SEO audit, there are basic, as well as comprehensive services when it comes to on-page SEO. At the most basic level, an on-page optimization campaign can be a one-time project which includes recommendations developed through an audit, and the implementation thereof. This type of on-page optimization would generally target the home page and a few other important pages on the website. More comprehensive on-page SEO campaigns will use the findings of a highly-detailed website SEO audit, and monitor results to guide ongoing changes to the on-page optimization. Even though on-page work does not need to be updated in many cases (e.g. when the site has evergreen content), it is recommended that the website and the content being published therein be audited on a regular basis to uncover potential problems which may creep up through website updates and changes.

SEO Content Development

SEO content development is the process of creating website content which can come in a variety of forms, including text e.g. articles, whitepapers, essays, research documents, tutorials, and glossaries, infographics (information graphics), PDFs, searchable databases, web tools, and the like. As you will note, the traditional definition of content is no longer appropriate, since content comes in many forms. It is also important to realize that depending on your niche, not every type of content would be suitable for your website.

'SEO content' is also a misnomer; content which can impact search engine friendliness positively should be more accurately described as "high quality content", which will in turn make earning and acquiring links much easier. When looking for content that is going to help your SEO efforts, it is crucial to look for high quality content; or more accurately, find people who can develop such content. Seeking out 'SEO content' can lead to content that is jammed full of keywords without much consideration for quality.SEO content writing as a service can be useful, if shortcuts are not taken, and the content is not expected to perform magic. Well written, interesting and useful content will inevitably be found, and get attention on its own merits; however, it also helps lay the foundation for a successful link development campaign.

Link Development

Link development is one of the most controversial and often talked (written) about topics of the SEO industry. Since backlinks are the most vital component of any SEO campaign, and at the same time the most time consuming and consequently most expensive (assuming they are good quality links and not just random directory submissions and blog comment spam) part, inevitably, there are many service providers who offer inexpensive link building services to attract and impress potential clients. Such schemes include large volumes of directory submissions (e.g., 200 directory submissions per month), worthless blog and forum comment spam (e.g., 100 blog links per month), or article writing and submissions which result in extremely poor quality content published on equally low-quality article directories which contribute in no positive way to ranking improvements. So if someone is quoting you a $500 per month SEO services which includes large volumes of directory submissions, blog posts, articles, blog/forum comments and so on, all you will be doing is throwing your money away. This is not to say that you can't get link-work for $500 per month; however, it won't be for a large volume of links.

Good quality link development work focuses on quality rather than quantity. A well-researched and relevant, good quality link is worth many times more than hundreds of free directory submissions. The fundamentals of link building are, have always been and always will be, based on good quality (i.e., useful, interesting, entertaining, educational) content. Because if there is no good content on your site that people can link to, it will be very difficult to convince them to do so.

Code Optimization

Code optimization is a service you can expect at the highest levels of SEO services, as it involves an overhaul of your website HTML. The optimization of your HTML can impact search engine rankings in two ways. First, it can help alleviate code-clutter, and present your content in an easy-to-understand (for machines, that is, search engine algorithms) format. Second, it can help reduce the load-time of your website pages, so that search engine spiders don't have to wait around while your page loads (because it's too long, or has too many images, etc). A comprehensive SEO campaign will have all the above elements, but it will also incorporate other important services such as keyword research, ranking reports, traffic reports, and conversion tracking.

SEO is important whether you're a seasoned ecommerce veteran or just starting to sell online. Optimizing your site will be a continuous process, as search engines are constantly surveying the internet to index and rank pages.

10. Tips for Optimizing Your SEO Strategy

No matter what type of marketing campaign you are working on, search engine optimization is the pivotal point in the success or otherwise of your plan. Unfortunately, the search engines are constantly making changes to their search algorithms, so how on earth are you meant to be able to keep up with it all?

The following advice and tips come from seasoned professionals, and are designed to help you find your way around SEO as the search engines constantly evolve. Make sure you are truly set up for SEO success by understanding the following points.

1. Document your strategy

As soon as you have finished reading this, get set and write your plan down. Your SEO strategy has to be documented, every single step. Start with a basic strategy and monitor it, then, when you have done some work on analyzing the results of your efforts, you can make the relevant changes. Having it all down in writing is absolutely vital for success; you can't possibly follow a plan without having it all laid out. SEO strategists who have their plan well documented are twice as likely to see success, compared to those who don't.

2. Your SEO campaign and content marketing campaign are partners, not opponents.

No doubt you already know of the so-called debate between SEO and content marketing, and I did touch on the differences earlier. There are agencies that specialize in one or the other, and they benefit from widening the gap between the two, however, this can be very damaging to your plan, and the success of your strategy. Content marketing and SEO are not in competition with one another. If you are coming up with content that supports your marketing goals and objectives, it should be fully optimized to increase the potential for your content to be located via the search engines. So, stop messing about and wasting time thinking about whether to opt for SEO or content marketing, use the two together and reap the rewards, whilst watching those who shun one in favor of the other fall at the first hurdle.

3. Make sure you audit your SEO progress

One of the first steps you need to take to improve your strategy is to audit your progress on your current SEO strategy. With the search engine algorithms changing on an ever increasing basis, it is vital that you consistently and regularly re-evaluate your plan. This is the only way you can possibly keep up with all the changes and continue moving forward - checking on your current progress is the only way to know where the improvements need to be made.

4. Think about the "4 Vs" of semantic search

Search is a personalized thing and that means that the traditional metrics of keyword and page ranking are no longer all that meaningful in terms of measuring SEO success. Searches are becoming more and more focused on semantics, or search context, and marketers have to change the way they evaluate their success. There are four components to semantic searches – volume, variety, velocity, and veracity and all of these should be incorporated into how you target your efforts, as well as how you promote them and measure your success.

A semantic search is a term that is often used instead of "contextual search", and it means "how the search engine discerns the context and the user intent, so that it can return definitive answers, instead of the usual hierarchical list of guesses that used to be presented." Confused? Put simply, semantic search helps the search engine to give the user better results.

When the search engine considers user intent, it means that two people who input the same search terms could get different results. These results are impacted by the location of the user, their search history, their social media networks, and so on, depending on the algorithm used by that particular search engine.

As well as considering user intent context, the search engines also try to incorporate the context of the content into the results as well. This means that search engines are moving away from keyword-driven searches, and are using meta data, like rich snippets, synonyms, and other information available on the site or page of the result, to determine whether a result is relevant to the user.

Finally, in terms of better results, search engines are returning results that are relevant and useful. Instead of just giving searchers a list of results, the search engines are trying to anticipate their needs and give them answers.

5. Use the right keywords

Although searches are heading towards being more context-driven, it is still important that you choose the right keywords, and use them in the right way. If you produce content for the Internet without thinking about keywords and search engine optimization, you will still rank for something, but you run a big risk of failing on your SEO strategy. Make sure that you research your keywords and use them properly, to gain the best results.

6. Optimize all of your content

As soon as you have your target keywords, you need to make sure that your content is fully optimized for them. Use keywords in the right concentration, and in the right places. The most important things to remember are to use your highest ranking keywords in your meta description, your content title, the first paragraph and the last paragraph of your content, and you must also ensure that your keywords are used in a natural way - not inserted into your content any old how. Your readers do not want to see content that looks or reads like spam.

7. Include SEO in your social media efforts

If you truly want to succeed in the world of sematic search, you have to make sure your social media efforts and your SEO efforts complement each other. That way, you are experiencing the best of both worlds and driving more, high quality visitors to your website.

8. Make sure you use the right SEO agency

Should you choose to go down the route of hiring a professional agency, you must make sure you choose the right one. You do not want one that sees SEO and social media marketing as polar opposites, nor one that separates content marketing out from the rest either. Instead, you want an agency who will use all of these strategies together, each complementing the other. Using an agency that favors one means a high possibility of ruining your chances of success.

9. Take full advantage of the SEO power of outside websites

One of the biggest parts of SEO success are inbound links from paid, earned, and owned media. One of the biggest successes in terms of outside sites comes from a website called Slide Share - one you have no doubt heard of.

Slide Share is search friendly, and that means when you post content on it, it is very likely to rank high on the Google SERPS. Any presentation that is posted on Slide Share is translated automatically to text, meaning search engines can find it easier than if the same content was on your own website. Use sites like Slide Share to leverage the power of your own SEO strategy, and to take your results to another level.

10. Make use of rich snippets

Rich snippets are a very powerful SEO tactic. They are a way of marketing your content in a way that lets the search engines enhance the results they display. There are lots of different types of rich snippet, including video previews, ratings, and images. The data makes the content far more appealing to the search engine and it can help you to get more clicks from the searchers, when it is displayed alongside the search listing. In short, they can make your content look much more enticing and more engaging to a searcher than a standard listing.

11. Don't forget to measure your success

When you no longer have just one set home page, it can be a little difficult to measure your success. However, there are several ways that you can gauge the success of your SEO strategy, as it ties to your content marketing strategy. One of the very best ways to do this is to use a tool like Google Analytics. This allows you to measure the true success of both your SEO strategy and your content marketing strategy, using different metrics to learn new things about your business, and see where any improvements need to be made.

12. Use SEO to improve all of your content marketing

While the constant changes in SEO and search engine algorithms can be somewhat frustrating, you should be happy about one thing - the wealth of data that is produced by your SEO strategy can be easily used to improve on your other marketing strategies. Using the free tools available, such as Google Analytics and Google Webmaster, you can build up a specific picture of how your overall strategy is working, and then apply the same to your other strategies. Don't forget to tie your content marketing and SEO strategies together for a boost in success.

Perhaps the most important step is that you should never stop learning about the power of SEO and how to do it properly; because SEO is ever-changing, there is always new information and new data coming out on a regular basis, which can help you to refine your strategy and improve your results.

How much revenue should you put towards your SEO needs?

We have talked at length about how important SEO is, whether you decide to do it yourself or you pay someone else to do the honors for you, but we know that money is not an endless pot; if your particular pot is endless, then you're very lucky indeed!

How much cash you should drive into your SEO strategy is a personal decision but you need to look at it sensibly. Yes, you need traffic to bring you business, in order for your company to survive, so that says that you need to be spending some cash on your SEO needs, but you shouldn't be overdoing it either.

Here are a few ways you can cut costs but still reap the plentiful rewards of SEO:

Basically do it yourself. If you're going to do this, make sure you know what you're doing. Research, read books, ask around for people to show you things, find someone you can trust who does their own SEO and ask for a few handy tips. This isn't something you can go into half-heartedly, so if you're going to do it DIY, make sure you can actually put the time and skills into the job. Look at it this way – if you were going to wallpaper your living room, you wouldn't simply buy what you think you need and soldier on hoping for the best, would you? Well, think of your SEO requirements as the same. Preparation and research is key.

Use more organic SEO methods than paid methods. This is probably the biggest money saver you will find, however it's worth noting that paid SEO is certainly something you should be taking advantage of to some degree. Look at your overall budget and set perhaps one quarter of it aside for paid SEO, such as AdWords, and make more use of free methods if your cash-flow is a little on the shorter side. It might sound like a total contradiction after you read the many paid SEO methods in this book, and why they are so important and effective, but at the same time, it's no good bankrupting yourself if you can't afford it. Be realistic – organic SEO is very effective too, and probably more authentic in many ways.

Write your own content. Using a freelancer is a great way to get quality content onto your website, because you're basically making use of someone else's talents, however if you can't afford to pay a freelancer, you're going to have to do it yourself. Not everyone is a writer, and it's not something that is particular easy, however having said that, it's not impossible either. Any content you write must be perfect in terms of language, spelling, and grammar, up to date, useful, relevant, realistic, creative, and attention grabbing. If you can tick all of those boxes, then you don't need to pay someone else to do it for you.

Manage your own website. If you don't know how to set up a website, by all means pay someone else to do the ground work for you, because the basics are something you need to get right, however once that is done, learn how to manage the site yourself, without having to pay someone else to do it for you. Again, read books, go on a course, research on the Internet, but arm yourself with the skills to do the job yourself, for free.

Remember that you do need to pour some cash into your SEO strategy, because it literally is the difference between success and failure. Having said that, you don't need to throw an awful lot of cash at it, because if you get it right, SEO will work for you, without major need to work too hard, to spend too much cash.

Think of it this way – if you spend too much money on your SEO needs, it's basically false economy, because anything you do make is going to end up backfilling the cost of your efforts!

11. Search Engine Services and Tools for Webmasters

Asides that the SEO community is actively involved in the creation and innovation of more tools to be used by organizations, businesses, and SEO professionals seeking to self-optimize, so many different services and tools are made available by search engines to assist webmasters during their SEO endeavors. For example, Google has different tools, advisory, and analytics content that is specially designed for webmasters searching for ways to have a stronger relationship with the search engine and that their websites are optimized in line with the recommendations of Google. After all, who can understand search engine optimization far more than the search engines?

Search Engine Protocols

Let us consider the different search engine protocols out there:

Robots Exclusion Protocol

The functions of this protocol are possible via the robots.txt file that is normally found in a website's root delivery. This protocol gives directives to automated spiders and web crawlers concerning the different issues like guiding bots as to where sitemap data can be found, the different areas of a site that are disallowed or off-limits, and shouldn't be crawled, and parameters given for crawl delay.

Below are the commands that could be used in instructing the robots:

Disallow: This prevents the robots from coming close to some folders or pages on a given website.

Crawl-delay: Crawl-delay provides the rate at which robots crawl pages on a given server.

Sitemap: With this command, robots will easily locate the sitemap as well as other files related to it.

Beware: While the vast majority of robots are compliant and nice, there are some of them whose design doesn't work in line with the protocol and therefore, will not follow the directives presently in the robots.txt files. These robots, at any time, could be used by dubious individuals to access the content they shouldn't have access to or steal private information. To prevent this from happening, the best move is to leave the administrative sections' address in the robots.txt file.

Also, you can use the Meta robots tag for these pages in order to inform these search engines not to crawl the pages. To analyze and access your website's search engine protocols, you can make use of the Google Webmaster tools.

Sitemap

A sitemap can be seen as a treasure map that leads search engines through the right path to crawl your website. With a sitemap, search engines are assisted in finding as well as classifying the contents found on a website, which could have been difficult locating on a normal day. There are different formats used in keeping sitemaps in. They can also reveal ways to different content forms, whether they are news, mobile, or audio-visual version files.

A tool referred to as XML-Sitemaps.com is used in creating sitemaps in an easy and friendly manner. Sitemaps come in three major formats:

• RSS

There has been a serious debate concerning if RSS should stand for Rich Site Summary or Really Simple Syndication. In terms of maintenance, it is quite convenient and can be coded, so they take on automated update properties coupled with the inclusion of new content. One downside of the RSS is that it is difficult to manage compared to other formats.

• XML

XML refers to Extendable Markup Language. When it was being created, someone decided that the XML sounds better compared to EML; this is how the initials got stuck. Most website design gurus and search engines recommend the XML format, and it's not surprising to see that it is also the most widely used. Being more passable by the majority of search engines, it is easily created by many different sitemap generators. Also, you'll have the best control of a page's parameters.

However, one disadvantage of this format is that the file sizes for these formats are usually heavy compared to some other formats.

• .TXT File

This format seems to be very easy to use, and for each line, it makes use of one URL and can go up to about 5,000 lines. The downside here is that it doesn't allow Meta elements to be added to pages.

Meta Bots

Meta bots can be used in giving instructions to search engine robots pertaining to just one page at once. This tag is usually included in the HTML file's head area.

The Nofollow attribute

As mentioned earlier, nofollow links help you link to a particular page without having to go through any linkjuice. Though search engines will stick to your wishes not to give any value to these links, they may end up following them for discovery reasons.

The Canonical Tag

You can end up with different URLs that cause similar pages of similar content. This may not be a big deal, but the repercussions are unhelpful for SEOs and site owners looking to enhance page value and ratings. This is because the search engines are yet to be very smart as we would want them to be.

This tag is used to inform search engines about which to count as 'authoritative' for result purposes. This helps search engines to comprehend all the versions of a specific page, and just one URL should be counted for the purpose of ranking while others have to be assimilated into it.

Myths and Misconceptions of Search Engines

Honestly speaking, we've all somehow heard of SEO legends, and even after being proved untrue and debunked, it still fills our minds with doubts. Below is a collection that may be of help in separating facts from fallacies.

Making Use of Keywords

This can be referred to as one of the most persistent and oldest fallacies of the world of SEO, and it seems invincible. This hidden truth of this SEO technique is that stocking anchor text, title, a page, and content with so many keywords is a special way of getting to the top of search engines. Sadly, so many SEOs still believe it to be true, and so many SEO tools stress the significance of the density of keywords and how they are used by the search engine algorithms. We are saying that this is false.

Keywords used with moderation, intelligence, and relevance are usually admired by search engines. Time shouldn't be wasted on the calculation of mathematical formulae as well as counting of keywords. Doing this will only annoy visitors and then make you look like a spammer.

Using Paid Results to Improve Organic Results

This can be called pure fiction. This never happened, and it is still not going to happen. Even countries that may be spending millions of dollars in search engine advertising may still need to fight or struggle over organic results, and no extra support is received by them or the slightest change in rankings when we talk of organic results, even when paid results are used.

Bing, Yahoo, and Google all have a strong separation between the departments to protect this type of crossover from happening and then risk the legitimate nature of the search engine machinery as a whole. If any SEO says he can do some magic regarding this, then get ready to take to your heels and run.

The Myths of Metatags_

We quite agree that, thus, used to true and worked effectively for a short time period, but for a considerable time period, it has failed to be included among the ranking's equation. Many years ago, search engines used to permit users to utilize the meta keyword tag while inserting relevant keywords from your content so that anytime the keywords of a user somehow match with yours, you would also come out automatically in the query.

However, the same category of people that played a role in the rise of the first myth utilized this method of SEO to the spamming overdose limit, and it wasn't long for search engines to regret whatever they did and get rid of this method from its algorithms. Therefore, be warned now, because this method has stopped working. Those referring to SEO as Meta tagging are obviously still existing in the previous decade.

The Measurement and Tracking of Success_

We've seen this as a universal management rule that anything that can be measured can also be changed. Though this doesn't hold true in all cases, it applies to the search engine optimization field. SEOs that are successful are known to use strong tracking and make use of measurement, which plays a significant role in success as well as the creation of better strategies.

Below are some of the metrics you'll want to track and measure regularly:

Traffic from Search Engines_

It is important to know the source of traffic that has contributed the largest share of traffic on your website every month. These sources are classified into four major groups which are based on the origin of the traffic:

- Direct navigation

These set of people typed in your website's URL and then came across your homepage, or those that have saved your website on their bookmarks, or those that were referred to your site by a friend on email or chat. Email referrals cannot be tracked.

- Referral traffic

This type of traffic refers to those visitors that came to your site after coming across some promotional content from links that are found all over the website or through some campaigns. These can easily be tracked.

- Search engine traffic (referred to as organic reach)

This refers to the query traffic sent by the search engines due to the searches made that show your website on the results page, and then the user visits your URL by visiting the link on the results page.

- Social traffic

This traffic has to do with the visits that come from social networks, which permits website owners to measure those benefits yielded by your efforts on the different social media platforms regarding visits and conversions.

Having some knowledge about the percentages and figures makes it possible for you to see where your strengths and weaknesses lie, to comprehend your decreases and increases in traffic, and its sources to pick up those performance patterns that may be illegible if you're not considering the larger picture with some segmentation.

Referrals due to some phrases or important keywords

It is very important to know those keywords that bring in the largest traffic, as well as those not performing up to expectations. Your website may be less optimized for keywords that normally should bring in lots of traffic and already contributes greatly to traffic.

Remember that, if your website comes as a song, then the keywords would be what everyone remembers, which will either be the memorable parts of the melody or lyrics. So, it is very important to know those keywords are doing for your website. The website's analytics are not complete without tracking the website's keywords performance on a regular basis. The good thing about it is that there are lots of tools out there that can assist you in keyword metrics.

Referrals by some search engines

It is very important to measure the performance of your website in relation to some search engines, not just the way your website is performing with search engines in general terms. Let's consider some reasons why having a picture of your relationship with some search engines is important:

• Comparing the share of the market against performance

This makes it possible for the traffic contribution of some search engines to be analyzed in line with their share of the market. Different search engines perform well in different fields of search categories. For instance, Google performs well in better areas characterizing more technology, Internet-literate, and younger population, in contrast to some other fields such as sports or history.

• Comprehending visibility graphs data

In the event of going into search traffic, if separate measurements can be kept of exact and relative contributions from some search engines, then it places you in a bigger and better position to locate where the problem lies. For instance, if there's a drop in the traffic and it is consistent across different search engines, then accessibility may probably be the issue rather than one having to do with penalties, where there'll be a larger drop in the contribution of Google compared to the others.

• Inquiring into strategic worth

Since some search engines respond in a different manner to optimization efforts, it is very easy to have a strategy that is focused and more effective in play, if it's possible to identify which optimization tactics or techniques are doing well for the search engine. E.g., keyword-centered methods and on-page optimization deliver results that are more significant on Yahoo! and Bing compared to Google. So you'll have an idea of what needs to be done to increase your rankings and attract some traffic from search engines and what might have been done the wrong way.

SEO Tools

Asides those tools mentioned earlier; several other tools can be mentioned as well, as they could assist website owners with different tasks regarding SEO, as well as measuring how your strategy came out successful.

The most significant of these tools are from Google – Google Webmaster tools (Bing has a similar tool designed those webmasters seeking to optimize websites for Yahoo! and Bing) and Google Analytics.

The main advantages of these tools are:

• This tool has a free version, which means anyone is allowed to make use of them. You only need a Google Account.

- It is easy to navigate, and therefore, even as a beginner, you'll have no problems making use of them

- They offer data that assists you with improvement in the usability of the website

- You'll have the opportunity to link to other services rendered by Google, like Google Ad Words, to help create a comprehensive report to improve and analyze the strategy's performance.

Webmaster Tools_

All webmasters should have this tool because it helps in analyzing and tracking a website's overall performance, structured data, crawl errors, internal links, etc. With your Google account, this webmaster tools can be accessed for free. Your website will have to be added to your Google Webmaster account to help you retrieve this information about your website.

Furthermore, this Google tool gives viable suggestions regarding your website's improvement concerning HTML improvements, which is very helpful when we talk of website optimization.

Some HTML improvements are:

- Missing title tag

- Missing meta description

- Too short or too long meta description

- Duplicate title tag

- Contents that cannot be indexed

- Duplicate meta description

- Too short or too long title tag

Google Analytics
This tool can be used in tracking a website's performance, visitors' behavior, sources of traffic, etc. Google Analytics delivers much data about your site, which can assist greatly in learning about those visiting your site (your audience), the ways in which they arrived at your site (acquisition), their manner of interaction (behavior), as well as the time spent by these visitors to your website. The activity can also be monitored in real-time and the conversions analyzed by linking to Google AdWords or setting up goals.

PageSpeed Insights

Since a website's loading time is a very significant factor affecting rankings, you should know about the speed of your website and make efforts to improve it.

When your website URL is analyzed, you'll get some suggestions that relate to the optimization of your website's different parts, which affects the speed of the website. These are:

- Image optimization
- Response time of the server
- Avoid redirects
- Prioritizing of visible content.
- Enables compressions
- Browser caching
- Gets rid of CSS or render-blocking JavaScript

This tool also offers suggestions on the best way to fix the elements.

12. The Importance Of Researching Your Competitors

When you're trying to rank for a keyword, you cannot underestimate the importance of researching your competitors. What your competitors are doing WILL and SHOULD strongly influence your own SEO strategy.

SEO isn't the kind of thing where you can say "oh, we'll just try it our way and see what happens".
Nothing will happen.

SEO requires you to scope out your competitors, see what they're doing, and **assess their strengths and weaknesses in detail**. This is how you find your "in" for the keyword you're trying to rank for.

With this in mind, here are some questions you should ask yourself when researching your competitors who are ranking for a keyword that you want to go after.

Who are my competitors?

First things first, who are you actually competing against?

This is an important question to ask, because if your top competitors are all well-known high-authority sites, you're probably wasting your time and money going after that keyword.

For instance, if I want to optimize a web page for "best makeup", a quick Google search shows me that the top 3 websites in the SERPs are:

- Elle
- Glamour.com
- Cosmopolitan

Now I'm all for optimism, but your cute little website is NOT going to take down Elle or Cosmo for a keyword like this - people trust these websites way too much and they're going to click on them over you most of the time.

Sorry.

Also, as discussed previously, having high website authority (which all 3 do) gives them a tremendous SEO advantage to begin with.

However, if you Google a slightly more specific keyword, such as, “best makeup for dry skin”, we can see that our competitors are:

- GoodHousekeeping
- Prevention.com
- Elle

While this would still be a fairly difficult keyword to rank for, the websites on this list aren’t quite so ridiculously high-authority in the beauty world (excluding Elle) so you’d have a slightly easier time ranking for this.

Ideally, we want something even more niche.

If we try the keyword: “best makeup for eczema-prone skin”, the top 3 results in the SERPs are:

- StyleCaster
- HealthCentral
- Makeup.com

Suddenly we’re not talking about big-name magazines like Elle and Cosmo anymore - these are **relatively unknown websites** that just happen to be ranking well for this niche keyword due to their good content.

In other words, this would be the easiest keyword to rank for out of the 3 examples because you’re up against competitors with lower domain authority that would be much easier to outdo.

Pick your battles wisely!

Why are they ranking well for this keyword?

We touched on this earlier a little bit, but it’s helpful to remember that there are **multiple reasons** that your competitors rank well for certain keywords.

Oftentimes a small blog website will be filled with detailed, in-depth, useful information, yet it gets outranked by a big-name publication (i.e. Cosmo) that offers a much worse article or page.

Authority goes a long way!

As a reminder, here are some of the things that can affect a website’s SEO score:

- **Website Authority** - how well-known and widely trusted is your site?

- **Meta Titles** - how well does your SERP title grab people's attention?
- **Meta Descriptions** - is your meta description relevant and keyword heavy?
- **On-Page Content** - is it engaging and well-formatted?
- **Web Design** - is your website nice and easy to use?
- **Backlinks** - how many other websites link to yours?
- **Page Load Speed** - is your website fast-loading?
- **Article Introductions** - does your intro pull readers in or not?

It takes some time and practice, but assess these factors in your competitors and try to figure out why they're ranking so well for a keyword.

Sometimes the answer isn't obvious, but over time you will get better at sussing out why websites are ranking for a certain keyword. Even if it's just for the fact that they load quickly and have a pretty UI, you should know.

What topics should I address?

Though the keyword you're trying to rank for will be the main topic of any high-ranking webpage, there are always **multiple sub-topics and related topics** that may be addressed within a webpage.

If these topics are relevant and useful to readers, then reader engagement is likely to be better (i.e. people stay on the page longer) and Google ranks the site well as a result.

For example, if you searched for "used cars Ottawa", you might find that some of the well-ranked results answer similar topics such as:

- Tips for buying a used car in Ottawa
- Average price of a used car in Ottawa
- What type of used car is recommended for driving in Ottawa?
- What is the most popular used car in Ottawa?

These things can often be found in the form of an **FAQs section** if they're not integrated into the copy/page itself.

By finding the topics addressed by multiple different websites and putting them into your content, you're providing a **one-stop-shop of useful content** that fills the content gaps of other pages in the SERPs.

Makes sense, right?

Essentially, you're taking the best of the best and combining them into something new - an **all-in-one crème de la crème resource** that's sure to outdo the competition and be incredibly useful.

And you know what Google likes? Pages that are useful and on topic!

How can I outdo my competitors?

Finally, you need to ask yourself how you can outdo your competitors.

But how?

Look at the top sites in the SERPs for the keyword you want to rank for. Every single website will have strengths and weaknesses, even if it's not obvious at first.

By assessing the strengths and weaknesses of your opponents while simultaneously being self-aware of YOUR OWN strengths and weaknesses, you can start to strategize a route to success where you blow them out of the water.

For example, you might look at your top 3 competing websites in Google and summarize the following:

STRENGTHS

- Good website authority
- Nice website UI
- High-quality photos
- Good formatting
- Strong backlink profile

WEAKNESSES

- Unengaging copy
- Content gaps
- Takes too long to get to the point
- Poorly researched

Unless you're pitting yourself against GQ or The New York Times, you'll probably be able to outdo your competitors by ensuring that you have engaging copy, fill in their content gaps, get to the point ASAP, and offer well-researched content.

This is ON TOP OF having as many of their strengths as possible - good website authority, strong backlink profile, nice website UI, good formatting, and high-quality photos.

You gotta be the best!

If you can get to the point where your webpage has **more strengths and fewer weaknesses** than their website does, you're more and more likely going to win the SEO race as readers engage with your page more over time.

13. 8 Common SEO Mistakes To Avoid

Though it's good to have a reference of what you SHOULD be doing when it comes to your SEO, it's also good to have a reference of things NOT to do as well.

Here are 8 common SEO mistakes you should avoid:

1. Starting without keyword research

This is one of the major mistakes that a lot of businesses make when starting out. If you don't figure out keywords that people are using to find businesses like yours, you are leaving money on the table.

Keyword research is the foundation of any SEO campaign. If you are a plumber in Austin and want to improve your presence online, you need to find keywords that people are using to find the services you offer and then optimize for those keywords.

Some of the most common search terms people use to find plumbing related services include:

- Plumber CITY_NAME
- Emergency plumber CITY_NAME
- Blocked drain CITY_NAME
- Toilet repair CITY_NAME

So make sure to perform in-depth keyword research to find out the right target keywords for your website.

2. Stuffing keywords into sentences weirdly

If you Google around, you can find plenty of websites that try to rank well for a keyword by stuffing it into their copy **too much and/or in unnatural-sounding ways**.

For example, it's not uncommon to see copy like this:

"Here at Bob's Plumbing, we're the best plumbers in Portland. We've been working in this region for the last 10 years, earning a name for ourselves as the best plumbers in Portland. When looking for plumbing services, you should look for the best plumbers in Portland, and that's us. So if you need to fix a leaky pipe or anything else, call Bob's Plumbing - the best plumbers in Portland - today!"

Take a guess, they're probably trying to rank for "best plumbers in Portland", no?

However, **Google is smarter than this** because **readers are smarter than this**. While pages stuffed with keywords like this can slip through the net occasionally, the writing will sound weird and unnatural to readers, often leading to lower engagement.

I mean, how annoying was that to read?

As discussed previously, keyword stuffing is penalized by Google, even if you work it into the copy more naturally. Shoving your keyword in at an unnaturally high density (i.e. higher than **1-2% density**) will not work, and it especially won't work if it makes your page sound dumb and annoying.

3. Ignoring the search intent of your readers

Search intent is a HUGE aspect of SEO these days, and ignoring it will not do you any favors. You need to consider what the searcher is ACTUALLY looking for when typing your target keyword into Google.

For instance, if they type in "best hi-fi systems", they're looking for a comparison of the best Hi-Fi systems on the market.

Yet strangely, many articles open with things like this:

"Hi-Fi systems are a great way to listen to music. Hi-Fis were popularized in the 1970s, offering people a way to listen to music in their homes. Hi-Fi systems come with speakers that allow you to listen at higher volumes than most devices.."

The person who's searching for this keyword **already knows what a damn Hi-Fi is**, and they're not going to be hooked in by an introduction giving them a definition of the thing they already know about.

A much better introduction would be:

"In this article, we've taken a look at the top 10 best Hi-Fi systems and compared them in terms of price, size, quality, and inputs. Our industry experts have looked at the pros and cons of each product, helping to choose the perfect Hi-Fi system for you."

This is great because it **matches the search intent.**

What this introduction conveys to the reader is this: "Hey, you already know what a hi-fi is and how it works, so let's cut to the chase. We're going to review the best hi-fi systems (as you expected) and this is what we're going to compare them on".

Straight away, the content of the page is lining up with the search intent of the user and they're able to quickly identify that this webpage is going to contain the information they need.

In other words, they're much more likely to stick around!

4. Focusing only on text

Although text is incredibly important for SEO, it's not the only way to improve your rankings.

For example, most modern web pages feature a combination of:

- Text
- Photos
- Videos
- Interactive elements (quizzes etc.)
- Slideshows
- Infographics

And much more.

While it's important to have text that flows well, is easy to read, and contains keywords... it's not always the be-all and end-all of your page.

If your competitors are making use of visual elements like video and infographics, it's a good sign that you should use similar elements too in order to keep readers engaged.

Just be careful not to put all your relevant keywords into photos, videos, and visual elements on the page - try to **include them as text in some places** so that Google still gets an idea of what your page is about.

Google is smart, but not THAT smart.

While machine learning algorithms have come a long way, most of them can't understand complex images and infographics yet, especially if they're nuanced in any way.

In other words, videos and graphics might improve your engagement with readers, but Google may not understand them.

5. Not optimizing your page/website for mobile traffic

As of 2020, mobile devices account for **50.81% of all internet traffic** around the world. As time marches on and smartphones and tablets become more popular, it's not unlikely that this percentage will grow even higher.

Long story short - there are **more mobile users** than desktop users.

This means that your page and your website in general need to be optimized for mobile traffic. If the desktop version of your website looks amazing while the mobile version takes a long time to load and has a poor user experience, you're going to lose around 50% of your visitors.

Depending on the keyword you're trying to rank for, you may have an even higher proportion of mobile users to take into account.

Some ways to better optimize your website for mobile traffic include:

- Improve your site's load time
- Make your mobile UI very intuitive
- Limit or get rid of pop-ups for mobile users
- Optimize for local searches (i.e. "flower shop near me")
- Keep meta titles & tags shorter (fewer words show up in SERPs on small screens)
- Actively create mobile-friendly content

Ensuring that your website implements these things increases your chances of optimizing for mobile users and ensures that a mobile visitor's UX is **just as good as a desktop visitor's UX.**

6. Not knowing your audience

Knowing your audience is the bread and butter of any experienced copywriter. Most writers will change the tone and style of their writing depending on the audience they're writing for.

For instance, if you own a law firm and you want to write a blog about "How To File a Personal Injury Claim", then the audience is going to expect **formal, objective writing**. If the copy is too informal, it can undermine the value of the copy and make your law firm seem unprofessional.

Not ideal.

However, if you own a small business selling cupcakes and you write a blog about "5 Perfect Cupcakes Ideas For This Summer", then your audience is **not going to be expecting anything serious**. Most likely your audience will be fun-loving parents and young adults who want to bake in their spare time.

In this instance, being light-hearted and informal makes sense.

It's useful to always keep your audience in mind in smaller, more subtle ways too. For example, if you're a man but you're writing a blog aimed primarily at women, you'll want to empathize with things from a female point of view and avoid referring to women in the 3rd person.

A lot of these things are incredibly subtle and hard to do if you're not an experienced writer, but that's where hiring a good team comes in handy.

Writing aside, knowing your audience also applies to other elements of your website!

For example, keep in mind how these factors will relate to your target audience:

- UI & color scheme
- The tone/style of the copy
- Font choice
- Pictures & graphics
- Attention span
- Layout etc.

If you've got a website aimed at young teens but the website has a boring color scheme and huge wall-of-text paragraphs, you're going to lose most of your website visitors very quickly.

However, if you made the website engaging, kept things short, and used visual elements to capture their attention more quickly, you're more likely to keep them on the site.

A lot of this stuff is common sense, but it's easy to forget.

7. Using irrelevant internal links

Internal links - using anchor links to promote other articles/pages on your own website - are a great way to build up your website and reinforce to Google what your website is about.

For example, if you were writing an article about The Best Tool Kits and you also had an article about The Best Hammers of 2021, you might insert a link like this:

"Tool kits are nothing without a decent set of screwdrivers and a solid hammer. In fact, this tool kit contains one of the best hammers I've ever seen and it works like a charm."

This is a good internal link - it fits, it's relevant to the main topic, and **it doesn't sound unnatural or forced.**

However, a lot of less-experienced writers and SEO specialists try to shove internal links into places where they don't belong.

Never forget the importance of **good anchor text!**

For example, if the same text had the same internal link placed like this:

"Tool kits are nothing without a decent set of screwdrivers and a solid hammer. In fact, this tool kit contains one of the best hammers of 2021 and it works like a charm."

While the phrase "solid hammer" is loosely related to the Best Hammers Of 2021 article, it's not close enough that it makes sense to use it as anchor text.

Also, **people should have an idea of what they're clicking on** and where it will take them - "solid hammer" doesn't suggest that it will take you to the Best Hammers page, it sounds more like it will take you to a review of a single... solid... hammer?

It's sloppy SEO.

Furthermore, you need to make sure that any internal links are closely related to the topics being discussed on your page.

For instance, if you're writing your blog about The Best Tool Kits and you included internal links to other pages such as "How To Clean Your Kitchen" and "5 Tips For Running Your Car In Winter", you're not necessarily helping Google to figure out what this page is about.

The more relevant and closely related your internal links, the better Google understands your website and what's going on.

In general, just make sure that your internal links make sense, have good anchor text, and won't mislead or annoy the reader.

8. Pleasing the Google algorithm a little too much

You can have too much of a good thing.

While SEO experts like ourselves are trying to "game the system" and force Google to like our content, it's not designed for us.

Google is designed primarily to find strong organic results. In other words, it wants to find web pages that "just happen" to be the perfect answer for the query typed into the search bar.

Too much obvious SEO can lead to **penalization** from Google.

Ultimately, you need to incorporate SEO techniques, but also know when to dial it down and keep the content feeling real and authentic. A perfectly crafted article with perfect keyword density, perfect layout, and perfect backlinks can look suspicious and be **too good to be true**.

Well, that's because it is.

Sometimes you need to just:

- Not optimize for every keyword perfectly
- Make the writing feel authentic
- Change up your anchor text (so it's not all the same)
- Get backlinks from some less-established websites
- Appeal to the reader and not the algorithm

If you loosen up your content and try to appeal to the reader a little more, this can often have the effect of boosting your ranking in the long run because Google recognizes that people are staying on your site, enjoying it, and reading your content.

So yeah, it's a weird push-pull situation.

Try your best to please the Google algorithm with the latest SEO guidelines and techniques we've discussed in this book, but don't make everything too perfect and remember to craft an enjoyable experience for the reader without shoving 50 backlinks and keywords in their face straight away.

If you can find this perfect middle-ground and adjust your pages based on their performance, then you'll be unstoppable.

The Bottom Line

We've covered a lot in this book. From the meaning of Search Engine Optimization to building backlinks, writing keyword-optimized copy, and using various on-page and off-page strategies to help your website appeal to both Google and your visitors, SEO is always evolving. But one thing remains true about everything else: make sure that you keep your readers engaged and satisfy their search intent.

While the guidelines and techniques used to "game the system" will always be changing and evolving as Google publishes new updates, the core tenet of SEO is that Google will reward good content that engages its readers.

Take the techniques discussed in this book and apply them to your business's website, but don't forget that your readers (i.e. customers) are the very reason you're doing this in the first place.

As the old adage says - the customer is always right.

Even if Google doesn't know it yet.

Extra - Building Backlinks Using Press Releases

If you're a new website or a website that's struggling to get backlinks, press releases can actually be a **godsend**.

Whether it's a company update, promotion, new product, or anything else, press releases may just be your new best friend.

And yes, this relates to SEO.

Why should I get a press release?

By sending out a press release that is **syndicated across multiple websites** across the internet, you can write your own article and include a link back to your company, as well as your NAP (Name, Address, Phone) information.

You see?

This is an easy way to **build backlinks and citations** from multiple websites, many of which have good domain authority. Press releases often get sent to **100+ media publications** online, so it's a great way to start establishing trust in Google's eyes.

It doesn't always work, but it's worth a shot.

Even if the citations and backlinks don't boost your SEO, you're going to inevitably raise your brand awareness and let more customers know about your business. It's a win-win scenario whatever happens.

BrandBoostr

If you're going to write a press release to help boost your SEO and brand awareness, I'd recommend using **BrandBoostr.**

This PR company extensively researches contacts at major publications and relates them back to your press release, combing through to find the contacts most likely to respond and publish your promo piece.

BrandBoostr **tailors your pitch to each media outlet,** ensuring that you maximize your chances of catching their attention and publishing your press release.

Some of the publications BrandBoostr has got people published on include:

- Forbes
- Reuters

- The Associated Press
- The BBC
- CNN
- The Washington Post
- ABC News
- Bloomberg
- USA Today
- Entrepreneur

And much more.

So if you think that this method of SEO and digital marketing would be beneficial in getting your website on the map, we highly recommend contacting BrandBoostr and speaking to a member of their team.

You could try to do all of this yourself, but ultimately, you need the **right contacts and industry know-how.**

Conclusion

By implementing effective SEO strategies and techniques, businesses can improve their visibility and ranking in search results and attract more potential customers. However, it's important to note that SEO is an ongoing process that requires regular review and updates in order to stay ahead of the competition and maintain your search engine rankings.

Effective SEO requires a deep understanding of how search engines work, as well as the strategies and techniques that are effective for improving a website's ranking in search results. Many businesses choose to hire an SEO expert or agency to handle their SEO efforts in order to maximize the chances of success and save time. However, if you have the knowledge and resources to do SEO yourself, it can be a cost-effective way to improve your website's ranking in search results.

SEO is a crucial aspect of digital marketing for businesses of all sizes and industries, and can be a powerful tool for attracting potential customers and increasing sales and revenue. By implementing effective SEO strategies and techniques, businesses can improve their visibility and ranking in search results and attract more potential customers.

Thank you for downloading my book. If you found it helpful, please take a few minutes to leave a review thank you.

www.ingramcontent.com/pod-product-compliance
Lightning Source LLC
LaVergne TN
LVHW082359200926
848481LV00012B/3617